COME REST WITH ME

EXPERIENCING INTIMACY WITH JESUS THROUGH GOD'S REST

Bryan R. Coupland

Copyright © 2009 by Bryan R. Coupland

Come Rest With Me
Experiencing Intimacy With Jesus Through God's Rest
by Bryan R. Coupland

Printed in the United States of America

ISBN 978-1-60791-368-9

All rights reserved solely by the author. The author guarantees all contents are original and do not infringe upon the legal rights of any other person or work. No part of this book may be reproduced in any form without the permission of the author. The views expressed in this book are not necessarily those of the publisher.

Unless otherwise indicated, Bible quotations are taken from The New American Standard Bible. Copyright © 1960, 1963, 1968, 1971, 1972, 1973, 1975, 1977, 1995 by The Lockman Foundation. Used by permission.

Cover photo by fine art photographer ©
M. Christine Duncan. Her work can be viewed at
www.c-duncans-photography.com

www.xulonpress.com

This book is dedicated to my dear wife Del, who has loved and served the Lord Jesus along with me all the years of our marriage.

"And He (Jesus) said to them (the apostles), 'Come away by yourselves to a lonely place and rest a while.' (For there were many people coming and going, and they did not even have time to eat.)"
                              Mark 6:31 NASB

ACKNOWLEDGEMENTS

Somewhere I heard that it is wise, when you have written a book and it is still in draft form, to have it read and critiqued by a broad spectrum of people you respect. I asked several dozen people to read the grammar-corrected copy and I am forever grateful for their input.

These friends include: Nancy Hamm, Tania Julin, Pattie Labutes, Gracia Burnham, Gene Miller, Doug Hefft, Oli Jacobsen, Arthur Franklin, Dr. Ken Royer, Dr. Lareau Lindquist, Henry Stewart, Patrick Brown, Dr. Richard Swenson, Dr. Laura Mae Gardner, Bob Wilson, Dr. Larry Copeland, Larry Brown, Rick Schatz, Andy Kline, John Cross, Joe Goodman, David Field, Debbie Waldoch, Dr. Doug Pennoyer, Ray Jones, Bill Meerstra, Jake Giesbrecht, Mel Wyma, Chet Plimpton, Dr. Mark McDonough, Duane Stous, Mike Sullivan, Pastor Vernon Rainwater, and our three children, Kelley, Terry, and Danny.

I am especially indebted to Rhoda Johnson and Pamela McGeorge, both freelance editors, who not only corrected the grammar but also shared many helpful ideas.

Andy Daniels and Doug Lotz applied their computer expertise to formatting the book into an acceptable digital form.

Many of the Biblical truths covered in this book are principles God taught my heart through faithful Bible teachers —

particularly NTM colleagues like Dave Calderwood, Chet Plimpton, Duane Stous, and Harold Tiegs.

My dear wife Del has worked so hard on this project with me, typing and retyping. There just would not be a book without her help and encouragement.

How I thank the Lord Jesus for His guidance in this labor of love! The principle of the believer entering into God's rest by faith is His truth, not mine. I have had the personal joy of writing about what God has designed for His children so they can abound in intimacy with Christ in a stressful world.

FOREWORD

Life is full of bumps and lumps. In the rough and tumble of everyday living, we often feel snowed under. We know from experience that hardships are not courteous—arriving one at a time, patiently waiting for us to recover from a previous trial. They tend to pile up. We feel besieged—stressed out. And, as if outside troubles were not enough, there is the added difficulty of what goes on within our souls.

But the Bible has the answers, right? Well yes, though often the Biblical answers seem to elude us. We may have been "born again" with Heaven our assured future, but life here on earth can be a bewildering mess.

As a young Christian I struggled with a sense of being chronically discouraged. I could never nail down why I felt the way I did. I had been raised in a good home, I had great friends, I had everything going for me, and yet I lived in spiritual defeat. My craving for the "victorious Christian life" made me vulnerable to spiritual doctors eager to write "Biblical" prescriptions for my heart. I launched into this and that, yet the abundant life promised in the Bible remained out of reach.

When I first met Bryan Coupland, he was teaching Bible in a missions training school where I attended. His lessons addressed many practical areas of life, sometimes touching on issues related to depression. I was keenly interested, but skeptical that anyone had an answer for my dark outlook on life. Besides, what Bryan was teaching sounded remarkably simple—too straightforward. Yet I could find no fault in his content—his careful exposition of the Scripture was sound. But did it work?

The answer to that question came in the normal humdrum of life. Another student and I were returning to campus one Sunday afternoon. It was a dreary day—heavy overcast, snowing, one step away from a full-blown blizzard—the sort of day that depressed people find depressing. We were talking about the lessons we were learning in class. I was sharing with him old Scriptures that had taken on new light—passages that I had never really understood before. In the process, I explained my struggle with discouragement and how I was hoping to someday escape its dark cloud. As we turned in the lane to the school it all of a sudden hit me. It was gone! When it had left me I could not really say, but my depression was gone! It had left my mind in such a way that I had not even noticed.

Was there some sort of "key" or "hidden formula" to escaping my gloom? No, not really. But often we miss abundant life and rest for the weary because we don't really understand how to appropriate the life and rest the Bible speaks about. We find ourselves living in a spiritual desert, with "peace like a river" in sight but seemingly beyond our reach. We know we are saved, but we struggle.

Bryan writes from the position of having been there. He humbly takes his years of Bible study and lays it out for all to read, simply and clearly. Though this book is scholarly, it does not come across as academic. Rather, it is written for those who need practical down-to-earth, "rubber meets the road" advice. It is meant to connect the dots, not only for those growing in their Christian life but for those who find themselves stagnating.

Because Bryan has sprinkled personal stories throughout the text, one has a gut wrenching sense that he is preaching what he has proven in the darkest hours of life—that there is a genuine rest for the believer. The "rest" he writes about is not theoretical, pie in the sky theology. It fits reality—those situations we all face in life. So read with thought and read with care. Don't miss it. You will be glad you took the time.

John R. Cross, Founder and General Director,
Good Seed International

INTRODUCTION

"I am sorry to have to tell you that there is a five centimeter tumor in your colon." The doctor had just completed my colonoscopy and I could read the concern in his face. I asked him if there was any chance it was benign and he just shook his head. Del and I sat there stunned. My mind went back four years to the last similar procedure when the doctor had said, "You shouldn't need another one for ten years."

We walked out to our car as if we were trying to wake up from a nightmare. When we sat down all we could do was weep and pray together. We had just crossed the threshold into a brand new chapter of our lives, populated with new terminology, testing procedures, and treatments.

The day I just described was April 11, 2008. I had finished writing my book and was correcting the grammar. I had also sent draft copies of the manuscript to a number of friends to critique.

One of my goals in writing about God's rest was to comment simply but thoroughly on a number of Bible passages dealing with this topic. I also wanted to interview four of the widows in New Tribes Mission whose husbands were kidnapped and killed by guerrillas. It is important for the reader to hear from the widows how God's rest was real to them in their excruciating experiences. I am very grateful that these women were willing to open their hearts and share the highs and lows of their experiences. Some of their quotes appear in the following chapters and the rest are in the Appendix.

When my head began to clear following the shock of the diagnosis, one of my first thoughts was, "Now that I've written a book about the rest God provides for His children, especially when they go through stormy trials, I wonder if He thinks it's time to test me in the laboratory of life." It's not as if Del and I have never encountered trials. During our ten years in Panama we endured an invasion by the U.S. military and later the kidnapping of three missionary colleagues. Shortly after moving back to the U.S., Del began to experience atrial fibrillation—she still has to take medication to keep her heart beating correctly. But this was a brand new area for both of us.

I have been a jogger for years and seldom thought about my health. Each year around my birthday I go for a medical checkup. Del and I also eat healthy foods. But now I'm immersed in a challenge that is completely outside my control. I am entirely in the Lord's hands. In reality, isn't this true for all of us all the time? It's just that certain situations make us realize our dependence on Him more.

The Bible passage that first came to my mind after the diagnosis was Matthew 14:13-34. The Lord Jesus had just fed thousands of people with five loaves and two fishes—much to the amazement of His disciples. Verse 22 says, "And immediately He made the disciples get into the boat, and go ahead of Him to the other side, while He sent the multitudes away." Shortly after, we read, "But the boat was already many stadia away from the land, battered by the waves; for the wind was contrary."

Why would Jesus send the disciples out on the lake when He knew a storm was approaching? Was it to demonstrate to them that the same God who fed more than five thousand people from one boy's lunch could also protect all twelve of them in the midst of a storm?

Come Rest With Me addresses the intimate relationship that Jesus Christ makes available for each believer who walks by faith with Him. Only in His rest can the child of God come to know Christ in a deep and personal way—only here has God's Son chosen to live His life out through him.

When Moses stood between the rebellious nation of Israel and an angered Jehovah God, he confidently petitioned, "Let me know Thy ways, that I may know Thee" (Exodus 33:13). What followed makes it clear that Moses' request pleased God.

King David described His desire for intimacy with God in Psalm 42—like a deer longing for water brooks. Earlier, in Psalm 27:4, he declared that the one thing he sought in life was, "to behold the beauty of the Lord."

There are many examples in the New Testament where this place of intimacy with Jesus is described in more detail. Matthew quotes the Savior saying, "Come to Me ... and you shall find rest for your souls" (Matthew 11:28-30). The disciple John wrote Jesus' own words that when the Christian believer abides (or rests) in Him, there is a whole list of benefits that are freely given (John 15:1-16).

The apostle Paul writes about the abiding rest of God throughout his epistles, filling in the picture from multiple angles. He appears to sum up all of his own life goals in this one poignant statement, "I count all things to be loss in view of the surpassing value of knowing Christ Jesus my Lord" (Philippians 3:8).

TABLE OF CONTENTS

Acknowledgements vii

Foreword.. ix

Introduction... xiii

1. José and Erlinda..19

2. Running in Circles in the Desert............................31

3. What's the Shortest Route to Canaan?...................39

4. Burnt Out and On the Run 49

5. The Saga of the Obnoxious Ox 63

6. How Can a Yoke Be Comfortable?..........................75

7. The Greatest Vine in the World.............................87

8. Fruit Growing—101...99

9. Going Out and Coming In—It's By Faith!............ 111

10. Don't Harden Your Spiritual Arteries! 127

11. Resting Sounds Good—But How Does It Work?..141

12. Christ In You, the Hope of Glory............................151

13. Finding God's Rest in the Furnace of Trial...........165

Appendix..173

Notes..183

Chapter 1
JOSÉ AND ERLINDA

José Maria Herrera is one of the most colorful men I have ever met. José and his wife, Erlinda, were our neighbors in the little Panamanian town of Chame about an hour-long drive west of the capital city. My wife Del and I would often go for a walk in the evening and we loved to pass the Herreras' home. It reminded us of a dollhouse surrounded by beds of flowers. Everything was neat, painted, and trimmed with care. Curiosity nudged us to the front door one evening. Our Spanish was not the best, but José and Erlinda raved about how well we spoke their language once we launched into our initial greetings and introductions.

I'm sure we shocked the Herreras that first evening with our visit. They graciously invited us inside and offered us something to eat and drink. It was as neat inside as it was outside and Spartan by U.S. standards. We explained that we were American missionaries working in their country with the goal of starting churches among the five indigenous people groups.

We learned that José and Erlinda were retired and that José had been a radio personality in Panama City. At eighty-one, he was still strong enough to ride his bicycle by our house every day. What a charming man he was, with a voice like the actor James Earl Jones. Erlinda, at seventy-nine, was small and frail and seemed ideally suited for their little dollhouse. In the course of the evening, I asked if they would be interested in studying the Bible with us. I'm not sure if they agreed out of fear or good manners, but we arranged to meet at their house on the following Monday evening at 7:00 p.m. for our first Bible study.

We soon discovered that Erlinda had been the religious focal point of the family for the sixty years of their marriage. When José didn't argue with her assessment of her religious steadfastness, Del and I filed that fact away as verified. José, on the other hand, had been a bit of a reprobate. Since he was fairly well known in his younger days as a radio personality in Panama, it was believable. I'm sure we only got a fraction of the total story on José's days of wine and roses. The looks that went between the couple signaled that there were many stories of anger, hurt, and starting over that would not be resurrected for our benefit.

During a lull in the conversation, I looked at José and said in my very best Spanish, "If you were to die tonight and suddenly find yourself standing before God, and He asked you, 'Why should I allow you into My perfect heaven?' what would you say?" I will remember José's answer as long as I live. With as much bravado as he could muster, he said, "I would tell God that I have kept *all* the commandments." Then he looked at his dear wife and asked with great seriousness, "There are *ten* commandments, aren't there?" If it wasn't such a deeply personal question, I think that all four of us would have exploded in laughter.

Here was a charming old man whose only hope for eternal life in heaven was keeping the commandments, which for him were buried somewhere deep in the Bible. He wasn't sure what they were or how many there were, but he was sure he had kept them all. I don't remember what Erlinda's reaction was to José's revelation, but the fact that she was able to keep a straight face would have given her my vote for an Oscar.

The only positive side to José's declaration was that it gave us a good idea where we needed to start in our Bible study: Genesis 1:1. There is much more to the Herrera's story, but I will finish it a little later. I share this much of their story to point out one consistent aspect of human nature that doesn't change from Greenland to Mozambique and back to Kalamazoo, Michigan. Men and women, regardless of the failure they know exists in their lives, still feel that God is so benevolent and understanding that He will allow them into heaven anyway when they die.

So, what does this story have to do with the topic of God's rest? Once we have the assurance from God's Word that we will live forever in the glorious presence of God, we learn that the whole fabric of the life of a Christian is wrapped around the wondrous truth of God's rest. We rest in God's promises for the assurance of eternal life in heaven, and then we rest in God's promises that He has provided all that is necessary for the Christian life on this earth.

Before digging more into this matter of resting, I would like to tell you another story: my own. José's story is about salvation and the need for him to rest in what Jesus had already done for him by dying on the cross. My story is about the role that resting plays once a person has received Christ's gift of salvation and begins to head out on the journey called the Christian life.

I grew up in Toronto, Canada, in a Christian home. In the first decade of my life, our family attended good Bible-teaching churches. I understood enough from church and Sunday school to know that I was not a Christian, so in my seven-year-old heart and mind I trusted in Jesus Christ. I can still remember my zeal for my street hockey buddies. I wanted them to know Jesus too.

This zeal for the Lord began to cool off as I transitioned into high school, where acceptance and popularity were more important to me. My parents had strict rules for me as I progressed through my teens, but I still managed to participate in my share of wrong activities. As I finished high school, I was a lukewarm Christian on the best of days.

College took me a hundred miles away from home and the independence made me feel like I was halfway around the globe. On the outside, I appeared no different than any of my fellow students who didn't believe in Christ. I knew in my heart I was a Christian, but I also knew that the choices I was making were displeasing to God. I quenched the Holy Spirit's conviction of my wayward lifestyle by telling myself, "God made me like this. I'm not like the quiet, reserved Christians." What a lie!

After college I began my career as a veterinarian, full of my own importance. I met my future wife, Del, ten months after I started my first job. Shortly before our wedding, Del also became a Christian. As I saw the changes that salvation brought to her life, I confessed my disobedience to Jesus Christ and returned to the joy and intimacy of a loving relationship with my heavenly Father. Del and I joined our lives together in a meaningful Christian ceremony.

I couldn't read enough good Christian books then to satisfy my hunger to learn more about my heavenly Father. I had braced myself for God's judgment and punishment for my disobedience; instead He broke my heart with His love and kindness.

Now that Jesus had my attention, I was determined to please Him. In my immaturity, I envisioned God sitting in heaven in front of a file cabinet—each Christian had a file. In His divine omniscience, God watched us closely every moment, and He would make notations in our files. I imagined God saying to Himself, "There is Bryan. He got up at 5:00 a.m. and read his Bible for an hour. That's worth two points. Oh no! He fell asleep praying. I'm going to have to deduct one of those points. He's trying at least. Now he's at work and he is thinking of talking about Me to his coworker. That's worth ten points. But he doesn't! Sorry, no points! He's daydreaming during that business meeting and it's not a wholesome picture. Sorry, Bryan; that's going to cost you eight more points. Did you know that you are in the negative figures for this week? Now he's angry at his wife for spending too much money. Bryan, why are you getting upset?"

So week after week, I tried my hardest to live the Christian life. I could keep it going for a while, in my estimation, but suddenly I would blow it on a grand scale. I would get so discouraged that I didn't seem to be moving forward. Trying harder only seemed to create greater frustration.

Sermons about the Christian's responsibility to work hard at living like Jesus did when He walked this earth did not lift my spirits. They only moved the finish line farther away. I was trying as hard as I could. I volunteered for everything possible at church, but it only made me feel like a hamster running on a wheel faster and faster without making any forward progress. Is this what God intended the Christian life to be; fighting the frustration of trying to be like Jesus and always falling short? Did being a good soldier mean that in this life you fight for all you're worth against the world, the flesh, and the devil, and then you go to heaven where God rewards you according to how well you held up with all the aggravation? Surely not!

I was a young professional with a lovely wife and a precious little daughter and yet I was totally frustrated with trying to please God through increased Christian activity. I was very sure that if this was how the Christian life worked, I was not tallying up a very good score. I had wasted a number of years in college living like an unbeliever and now I wanted to somehow make up for the lost time. I was serious about pleasing God and yet my life seemed less restful than ever. I was reading my Bible and praying what I felt was a considerable amount of time. Something wasn't connecting. I can remember thinking, "How much is *enough* prayer and Bible reading? Can a human being ever reach enough?" I would even make plans to do more of these good things, but the first morning that I slept through the alarm I felt crushing defeat. A friend gave me an excellent book called, *The Saving Life of Christ*.[1] The author, Major W. Ian Thomas, explained simply and clearly what God says in His Word about living the Christian life by faith. God the Holy Spirit drove the truth home to me. My striving heart was worn to a frazzle and I was ready for God's rest. That was thirty-eight years ago. I can still remember the exhilaration and joy of that heavy load of trying to be like Jesus rolling off my shoulders and onto the outstretched arms of my Savior.

*   *   *   *

I would like to finish the story of our Panamanian friends, José and Erlinda Herrera. It was evident from almost the beginning of our studies that José was counting on having kept the commandments in the Bible for his salvation, even though he wasn't sure what they were or how many were actually on God's list.

We gave our friends a Spanish Bible and we observed that the deeper the four of us got into the study, the more José cherished his Bible. Erlinda was very cautious at first, probably for several reasons. She had undoubtedly done her best to hold her family together around their religious traditions, and now in her late seventies, she and José were seriously studying the Bible with *gringos* from down the street. Erlinda's concern was understandable since she barely knew us and her husband was taking increasing interest in what we were teaching.

We tried to meet at least two evenings a week. I began in the first chapter of Genesis and then taught chronologically through the Old Testament. José had all kinds of questions and comments. Little by little we studied our way through the story of creation, the fall of Adam and Eve, the serpent, and Cain and Abel. We discussed Noah and the Flood, the Tower of Babel, and the life of Abraham. I emphasized our spiritually lost condition because of the sin of our first parents and also our own sin, but pointed out God's continual promise of a remedy for that sin beginning with Genesis 3:15. I explained that the shedding of blood as an offering for sin pleased God and that He shed the blood of animals to provide clothing for Adam and Eve. We studied further examples of that principle in Abel's offering, Noah's offering, and especially in Abraham's willingness to offer his only son. We covered the high points of Genesis, constantly emphasizing man's sinful condition, God's perfect holiness, and God's promise of a solution to man's problem. As might be expected, José could not at first put all the parts together to see the whole picture. Erlinda continued to listen carefully without much comment.

After about twenty studies, the four of us were sitting around the Herreras' kitchen table one evening and we started reading the book of Exodus. I was anxious to talk about the Ten Commandments, since this appeared to be the Mecca of José's religious worldview. We talked at length about how God instructed Moses to paint the door posts with the blood of an unblemished lamb. His eyes never left mine as I explained the symbolism of this highly significant sacrifice. José was straining to catch each explanation now. He would repeat different phrases and parts of verses in that deep resonant voice, as if savoring the truth in each word.

We next studied the Exodus of Israel and the giving of the Ten Commandments by God to Moses. I went over each of the Commandments in detail to make sure the Herreras understood why it appeared to be so important to God. I emphasized the fact that Jesus clearly said in the Gospel of Matthew that He was just as concerned if we savor the sin in our hearts and minds, as if we do it overtly where others can see it: "You have heard that it was said, 'You shall not commit adultery'; but I say to you, that everyone who looks on a woman to lust for her has committed adultery with her already in his heart" (Matthew 5:27–28).

It was a sobering moment for José when I told them, "I'm not proud of it, but in my own life I have, at one time or another, broken every one of the Ten Commandments, either in my mind or as an action." Verse after verse seemed to chip away at José's self-righteousness. What the Holy Spirit seemed to use to drive home the point of his utter hopelessness was when we read in the Epistle of James, "For whoever keeps the whole law and yet stumbles in one point, he has become guilty of all" (James 2:10). José wasn't just responsible to keep more than half of the Commandments. God was saying that if we slip and do wrong in even just *one* area (a virtual impossibility) then we become responsible for breaking the *whole* law and will be appropriately punished by God.

After going back through and explaining each of the Ten Commandments a second time, I said to José, "What thoughts do you have, my friend, about being able to keep *all* of God's Commandments?" As long as I live I will remember the expression on José's face and hear his desperate conclusion. He looked at me like a child who had lost his parents in a department store and didn't begin to know where to look for them. Lost! Hopeless! Fearful! José said in his deep, haunting voice, "*We are all lost!*""

Isn't that really the purpose of the commandments of the Old Testament? Isn't that partially why God gave Israel an endless string of laws that governed almost every area of their lives, so they could see that it was impossible for them to please God through their own efforts? At Mount Sinai the children of Israel brazenly told God, "All that the Lord has spoken we will do!" (Exodus 19:8). José had said basically the same thing but now the spiritual bill had arrived. José was stunned and his watery brown eyes mirrored the panic in his soul. For eighty-one years he thought he had kept all of God's commandments and now he had suddenly learned from the Bible that he was guilty before God of breaking them all. José had enjoyed a measure of confidence in his own goodness and God's Word had swept it all away.

We continued our study through the rest of the Old Testament. José was a different man now from our first meeting. He was less like a cocky, self-righteous man of the world and more like a nonswimmer who had fallen out of a boat and desperately needed a life preserver. He was beginning to see the picture accurately that before God, he was *eternally lost*. That was pretty much José's state of mind as we finished the Old Testament and started into the New Testament. Erlinda continued to be quiet but attentive to every comment and verse of Scripture. By now, José realized that God was infinitely holy and that he himself was a lost sinner, totally undeserving of being in heaven with a holy God. However, he also understood that because of God's love for mankind, He had provided a remedy that involved the shedding of the offering's blood. You could see the spiritual fog beginning to clear—like the sun burning the morning mist off a lake—as we began to read the New Testament. The life preserver that José longed for came to him in the words of John the Baptist. When John saw Jesus coming toward him, he said those soul-satisfying words, "Behold, the Lamb of God who *takes away* the sin of the world! [emphasis added]" (John 1:29). It was all about what Jesus had done!

However, the verse that really nailed it for him was, *"For God so greatly loved and dearly prized the world that He [even] gave up His only begotten (unique) Son, so that whoever believes in (trusts in, clings to, relies on) Him shall not perish (come to destruction, be lost) but have eternal (everlasting) life (The Amplified Bible)*" (John 3:16).[2] In the simplicity of this verse that so many children memorize and sing, he finally saw himself going down for the third time and Jesus Christ being there as his spiritual life preserver. José had been born again and this verse was his theme song! He would ride his bicycle by our house in the early evening and when he didn't have time to stop and talk, he would yell out, "*Juan tres, diez y seis!*" which in English means, "John 3:16!"

We believe Erlinda also trusted Christ as her Savior—she just wasn't as verbal as José. We talked to her at length about salvation by grace through faith alone and she made it clear that she was trusting only in Christ's shed blood for her salvation. Within the year, Del and I were transferred back to our mission's U.S.A. home office in Florida. I would call our dear Panamanian friends by phone from time to time. José was well into his eighties by then and when I would tell him who was calling, he would start crying. I was his spiritual father even though he was thirty years my senior. God's grace had made his heart so tender. Erlinda passed away shortly after our transfer and José moved into a nursing home in Panama City. I continued to call José and as soon as I identified myself on the phone, you can guess the first words out of his mouth. You could hear the smile in his voice as he repeated his precious Bible verse, "*Juan tres, diez y seis!*"

CHAPTER ONE – THEMES FOR FURTHER STUDY

INTRODUCTION

When I finished writing this book, I went back through it and picked out what I believe are the most significant *themes* related to the topic of God's rest. This study guide can be used effectively in your personal Bible study, a Sunday Bible class, a home (small group) Bible study, or as a tool for discipleship. It is my earnest desire that this guide will expand your personal study of God's Word, give you a deeper appreciation for God's rest, and most importantly, cause you to grow in your knowledge of Jesus Christ.

SUGGESTIONS FOR HOW TO STUDY

1. Read the theme several times by itself and, if necessary, read it in the context of the book chapter. Look up the Bible verse at the end of the theme and meditate on it.

2. Does the theme represent what you understand that Bible verse to mean?

3. Underline the key words in each theme and make sure you understand them.

4. Make a list of any other verses that could shed further light on the meaning of that particular theme. A concordance can be a great help here.

5. Write out questions that come to your mind as you read each theme with its Bible verse.

6. Because God's Word is *truth*, all the themes of the Bible are integrated in a consistent way. Are there other topics or doctrines that stand out to you that could be integrated with God's rest, as described by this theme?

7. In chapter twelve, there are questions rather than themes. These can be answered and developed further as you prefer.

THEMES

- To become a Christian, we must rest by faith in God's gracious promises in Scripture that He has provided all that we need for eternal salvation. He sent His Son, Jesus Christ, to earth to die on the cross in our place to pay for our sin. Following His death, He was buried and after three days in the grave was raised again to life. (Ephesians 2:8-10)

- To mature spiritually as Christians, we must rest by faith in God's gracious promises in Scripture that He has provided all that we need for life and godliness. (2 Peter 1:2-4)

- The Christian life is *not* about us doing as many *good things* as possible (like keeping the Ten Commandments), nor is it about trying to imitate the life that Jesus lived here on earth. Both approaches are impossible! (Titus 3:4-6)

Chapter 2

RUNNING IN CIRCLES IN THE DESERT

It could be called one of the greatest athletic disappointments ever seen on television. The year was 1984 and the event was the summer Olympics. Mary Decker of the U.S. track team had missed the 1976 Olympics due to injuries; four years later the United States boycotted the Moscow event. Finally, after more than eight years of training and preparation, Mary was ready to run the ladies 3,000-meter race. Considered the favorite, she was at her physical peak. This was her time to claim her gold medal and go down in athletic history as a champion—a household name. Also running in the 3,000-meter competition was a youngster from South Africa by the name of Zola Budd. She wasn't even wearing track shoes, but instead ran in bare feet.

I remember watching closely as the runners took off at the first sound of the gun and started around the first turn of the track. As I recall, Mary was ahead of Zola but as the teenager edged up behind the veteran, their legs became entangled—Mary went spiraling into the infield and came to a very awkward stop. Zola kept going with the pack. More stunning than even the fall was the look of horror, anger, and devastation on Mary's face as she watched the other runners, including Zola, continue around the oval. It seemed like they never noticed she was gone. The look on Mary's face was one of excruciating disbelief.

There is a Bible verse that I have come to greatly appreciate and every time I read it, I think of this particular Olympic 3,000-meter race. Galatians 5:7 says, "You were running well; who hindered you from obeying the truth?" When we find that we are not experiencing God's rest, it can be tempting to blame other people or our circumstances for the anxiety in our hearts.

A very sobering event occurred in Israel's history not long after God had miraculously delivered the nation from bondage in Egypt. He had parted the waters of the Red Sea making it possible for fleeing Israel to cross on dry ground. Subsequently, Pharaoh and his army drowned. You may not be as familiar with the conversation that God later had with Israel at Mount Sinai before He gave them the Ten Commandments. Exodus 19:5 records God saying, "Now then, if you will indeed obey My voice and keep My covenant, then you shall be My own possession among all the peoples, for all the earth is Mine." You would expect Israel, who had recently faced annihilation by Pharaoh, followed immediately by God's miraculous delivery, to fall on their faces in humility and love for their wondrous God who had just declared them His special nation. Their answer, however, is rather typical of well-meaning human nature: "And all the people answered together and said, 'All that the Lord has spoken we will do!' And Moses brought back the words of the people to the Lord" (Exodus 19:8).

Did God say that this was exactly what He was hoping His people would say in response? No, because He realized the pride and self-confidence in their promise. Sadly, verse 9 reads, "And the Lord said to Moses, 'Behold, I shall come to you in a thick cloud'." This was not the intimate presence of

God with His covenant people but rather God in His infinite holiness hidden from His rebellious children by a thick, dark cloud.

We are familiar also, with what took place after this exchange in chapter 32 of Exodus, while Moses was up on Mount Sinai receiving the Ten Commandments from God. Under Aaron's direction, the nation of Israel took up a gold collection and fabricated a calf. Not satisfied with that sacrilege, they brought offerings to their molten animal. Aaron, Moses' brother, further incriminated himself by saying, "This is your god, O Israel, who brought you up from the land of Egypt" (Exodus 32:4). The same ones who had earlier promised God that *all* that He said to them they would do, now "Sat down to eat and to drink, and rose up to play" (Exodus 32:6). We can only imagine what that was like!

All that I have mentioned to this point leads to the climax in chapters 33 and 34 with countless insights into God's character. God had every right to be angry with Israel. We begin to get a sense of the degree of God's anger when in the midst of giving the Ten Commandments to Moses on Mount Sinai, even while the partying was going on down below, we read, "Then the Lord spoke to Moses, 'Go down at once, for *your* people, whom *you* brought up from the land of Egypt, have corrupted themselves' [emphasis added]" (Exodus 32:7). Israel is about to experience God's righteous anger. Then later He instructed Moses, "But go now, lead the people where I told you. Behold, My angel shall go before you; nevertheless in the day when I punish, I will punish them for their sin" (Exodus 32:34).

God promised Abraham (then called Abram) He would give to his descendants the land of Canaan (Genesis 12:7). However, God's promise of His abiding presence was conditional on Israel's obedience to Him and they had just demonstrated that this was the farthest thing from any of their minds. So, God told Moses that His angel rather than His own glorious presence would accompany Israel on their trip to Canaan. Then He gave further explanation: "Go up to a land flowing with milk and honey; for I will not go up in your midst, because you are an obstinate people, lest I destroy you on the way" (Exodus 33:3). What was the reaction of the revelers and partygoers? "When the people heard this sad word, they went into mourning, and none of them put on his ornaments" (Exodus 33:4). No one was thinking of playing at this point. God added, "Now therefore, put off your ornaments from you, that I may know what I will do with you" (Exodus 33:5). There may be a little irony in God's comment because many of the Israelites had already contributed all their ornaments to make the golden calf.

In my own family, after being caught in a lie, my mother told me to go into my bedroom and wait while she decided on my punishment. Can you imagine God telling Israel to take off their party clothes while He decided on their punishment? Just thinking of all the options that God had at His disposal is enough to give anyone a panic attack.

In the midst of these dramatic verses dealing with Israel's disobedience and God's impending punishment is a sensitive verse that describes the intimacy Moses experienced with the God of Israel. It also has an important bearing on what happens next in the story. We read, "Thus the Lord used to speak to Moses face to face, just as a man speaks to his friend" (Exodus 33:11). In Numbers 12:7-8, we get an even more tender description of Moses' relationship with God, "Not so, with My servant Moses, he is faithful in all My household; with him I speak mouth to mouth." What an amazing claim for the Creator of the universe to make about a human speck on tiny planet Earth! But it speaks volumes of the intimacy that Moses, a shepherd of God's flock, enjoyed with his heavenly Father.

In Exodus 33 we are allowed to listen in on a most amazing discussion between Moses and the God of Israel.

Read the second half of this chapter slowly. The first half is flavored with God's anger and impending punishment, but the second half sounds like it's happening in a different time and place. As you savor the latter passage, you will discover some thrilling aspects of God's nature. Given God's statements in verses 3 and 5 of Exodus 33, you would think Moses would feel like a whipped puppy cowering before God, waiting for the verdict to fall. I believe that because of the love relationship described in verse 11 that Moses had with God, he felt the freedom to talk frankly with God—not as equals, but as one who understood the heart of the other.

Moses starts out by saying to God, in so many words, "You told me to lead the nation of Israel, as rebellious as they are, up to Canaan. But You have yet to tell me *whom* You plan to have accompany and protect us." Moses then makes a bold statement. He reminds God (who in His omniscience needs no reminding) of two very important promises that He has made. The first is, "I have known you by name" (Exodus 33:12). Doesn't God know everyone by name? Of course He does. I believe that Moses is speaking of the close friendship that he enjoyed with God. Moses was stating that he truly valued this unique relationship with his heavenly Father and we can see that this pleased God. Moses' second statement is even more profound. He reiterates to God that He had told him clearly, "You have also found favor in My sight" (Exodus 33:12). The more solid a love relationship is the more respectfully bold one can be to articulate it.

It's very important at this point to recognize that Moses does not try to debate the fine points of God's commandments: "Now God, You didn't specifically say anything about gold calves made out of people's jewelry!" Moses knew that Israel had turned their backs on the very one who had rescued them from the brutal hand of Pharaoh and his army. Then Israel had given in to their basest desires, totally ignoring God's holiness. Moses appears to reach beyond the letter of the law and grasp the principle of God's grace. In Exodus 33:13, Moses seems to be saying to his heavenly Father, "As a holy God, whose righteousness has been terribly offended by Israel, You have every right to be angry and in Your justice to destroy every last remnant of the Hebrew nation. Although Your perfection demands justice, I believe that Your heart delights in mercy and grace. So I appeal now to Your grace."

The law of God does not rest on the foundation of relationship like grace does. Therefore Moses appeals to God on the basis of the relationship he has developed with his heavenly Father. The power of God is seen through His *justice* but the beauty and glory of His character is seen through His *grace*. Moses continues to advocate for Israel by reminding God of His love and favor. He points to what I believe is God's heartbeat for mankind—that men, women, and young people would pursue a deeper love relationship with Him, longing to understand His personality and nature.

I don't believe that Moses was attempting to be an artful attorney here. God knew the heart of Moses better than anyone. He knew that this leader of Israel loved Him for who He was—love and grace personified. Moses' words resonated with the same chords that God's heart did when he said, "Let me know Thy ways, *that I may know Thee* [emphasis added]" (Exodus 33:13).

Yes, God is looking for people on every continent on planet Earth who want to know Him in ever deepening ways. 2 Chronicles 16:9 draws a vivid word picture for us: "For the eyes of the Lord move to and fro throughout the earth that He may strongly support those whose heart is completely His." Isn't that encouraging? Can you picture God constantly looking all over the earth, checking people's hearts as He goes? What exactly is God looking for? He is searching for people whose hearts are completely His! Why? So that He can strongly *support* them. If someone is going to support me, I want it to be the one who spoke the entire universe into place in mathematical precision.

In Exodus 33:13, Moses acknowledges that Israel has sinned and has no excuse whatsoever. Nothing has changed Moses' intimate relationship with God. In fact, he wants to know and understand God more deeply. It appears that Moses is heartbroken because God will not accompany Israel up to Canaan—he doesn't want to go without God. He reminds God, "Consider too, that this nation is Thy people" (Exodus 33:13). What will be God's answer to Moses' appeals? In my Bible I have to turn the page to read God's response, and this only heightens the drama. He would have every right to say, "Moses, you are forgetting My holiness. I do love you but these scoundrels have worshipped a calf of their own making, so now is not the time to be talking about our relationship. Stand aside!"

Unless you recall reading these verses before, God's response ought to floor you. You can almost see a huge smile breaking over God's divine face as He claps His holy hands together and shouts in His thundering voice, "My presence shall go *with you*, and I will give you *rest* [emphasis added]" (Exodus 33:14). How does that make you feel? If you and I know Jesus Christ as our Savior, this is the same heavenly Father with whom we are going to spend eternity. Does God's response surprise you? Was He not bent on punishing disobedient and ungrateful Israel? Didn't God say to His covenant people that He would not personally accompany them to Canaan because in His righteous anger He might destroy them along the way? Now God is jubilantly promising not only to accompany Israel but also to bring them into His divine rest. What caused the apparent change in God's attitude? What does He mean by saying He will accompany Israel on what turned out to be a painful forty-year trip to Canaan? What does God mean by promising to bring them into His rest? Was this rest to be in the near future? Would it happen when Israel reached Canaan? Or was God speaking of the time when the Israelites who trusted in Him would enter heaven? I believe that the answers to these questions lie in the remainder of God's Word and in the subsequent chapters of this book.

CHAPTER TWO – THEMES FOR FURTHER STUDY

- When the nation of Israel told God that they would do *all* He wanted them to do, it reflected their pride and arrogance rather than their loving obedience. (Exodus 19:1-17)

- Although God's holiness requires Him to deal with mankind in *justice,* He also delights in extending *grace* and *mercy* to us. (Psalm 103:1-17)

- God's grace rests on the principle of Him initiating and developing a *relationship* with mankind. His Law is a unilateral divine code of commandments that mankind is obliged to obey. (Exodus 33:11)

- God longs for people of all ages to seek a deeper love relationship with Him, to know Him more intimately, to depend on Him for everything, and to make each activity an act of worship. (Psalm 5:11-12)

- God is pleased when we tell Him that we want to know Him and His ways. (Exodus 33:13)

Chapter 3

WHAT'S THE SHORTEST ROUTE TO CANAAN?

Before we continue with this very meaningful discussion between Moses and God, let's return to the topic of running. I would like to think that I am a runner. Realistically, I am more of a jogger. I hope that I'm helping my cardiovascular system—I know that I am learning some wonderful lessons about the Christian life. Just completing a 5K race is reason enough to celebrate—even before the endorphins kick in.

I am beginning to see why the apostle Paul used the topic of running as a picture of the Christian life, because there are so many similarities:

- WHY RUN? The most obvious reason is that it is good for the heart and lungs. I'm hoping that jogging will maintain my physical quality of life so I'll still be able to shoot baskets with my grandsons after I retire. I also need the discipline of running. I have an inborn tendency to want to quit before completing a task, so finishing a distance that is taxing for me

is character building. The parallel with the Christian life ought to be obvious.
- RUNNING'S ENEMY – How does running impact you? Do you find that the constant repetition and exertion can quickly make it boring? Before you know it, running has become plain hard work. Our bodies are programmed to stop doing something that is painful, like hitting your thumb with a hammer. So the natural tendency when I get to the huffing and puffing stage is to want to stop doing it—*now!* I know I'm going to feel so much better if I stop. The Biblical application is clear where we read, "Knowing that the testing of your faith produces endurance" (James 1:3). The word *endurance* literally means staying-in-underpower. Although I don't like the tribulation, I know I need to develop the patience that it produces.
- THE MIND – I believe that the battle to finish is not won or lost in my legs or in my lungs, but in my mind. Especially between miles two and three, I can't think of any good reasons to keep inflicting such punishment on myself. My mind keeps shouting, "Stop running then!" My legs still have some strength left, but my mind wants to quit. It is so easy to rationalize sitting down at that point.
- THE SHORT TERM FOCUS – When you are running to train, the immediate goal is to finish what you set out to do. At the end of a 5K race, win or not, there is a great feeling of accomplishment—and besides, the snacks are free at the finish line! Some runners say that they break their run into a series of smaller, achievable distances—for example, to a particular tree or to the end of the block.
- STOPPING IMPETUOUSLY – There are times when I realize I have unconsciously slowed down and started walking instead of running. We can do

that in life too, can't we? Some pressure or stress creeps in and without giving it thoughtful prayer, we realize that we have backed away instead of proactively tackling the problem.
- PERSEVERING LONGER WITH AN ENCOURAGER – I have run in 5K races when my wife was there and when she was not there. I much prefer it when she is a spectator. Otherwise, I arrive at a race by myself and don't really know anyone. No one cares whether I do well or not—in fact if I drop out, they are farther ahead. However, when my wife Del is there and I catch glimpses of her during the race, it's a tremendous boost for me. In my last race she was standing at the finish line but I couldn't see her until the last three hundred yards. I knew she would be cheering me on like a champion, even though more than a hundred runners had already crossed the finish line. How could I quit? There is a tremendous picture here of being an encourager— helping our fellow believers to finish the Christian life strongly. Maybe this is what Philemon 7 means, "Because the hearts of the saints have been refreshed through you, brother."
- TRUSTING THE LORD – I would like to think that I can routinely run 5K (3.1 miles) myself, but each time I go out, whether it's a training time or a race, I end up praying, "Father, I can't make it! I really want to quit! Please help me to finish!" And He does!

The journey of the nation of Israel from the Red Sea to Canaan is very similar to a foot race—a very slow race that took Israel forty years instead of two to four weeks. When we last looked in on them, Moses was once again interceding for them before Almighty God. In Exodus 33, God told Moses, following the golden calf incident, that He would send an angel with the people of Israel up to Canaan but He Himself would not accompany them. Twice He said that if He was there with them He might destroy them all. But Moses reached beyond God's law, which Israel was guilty of breaking, to the grace and mercy in which God delights. In verse 13, Moses said to God, "If I have found favor in Thy sight, let me know Thy ways, that I may know Thee." As the intercessor for His people, Moses finished by saying, "Consider too, that this nation is Thy people." How did God respond to Moses' request? We can almost hear God answering with a thundering affirmation and visualize a huge smile on His face with His divine arms outstretched, saying, "My presence shall go with you, and I will give you rest" (Exodus 33:14).

Can you sense God's joy and pleasure with the words that Moses said to Him? How different Moses' attitude was from that of Israel. They foolishly had told God that they would keep whatever commandments He would give them. What blind arrogance! Moses, on the other hand, demonstrated why God said of him, "Now the man Moses was very humble, more than any man who was on the face of the earth" (Numbers 12:3).

Moses then makes a profound statement which I think he believed with all his heart: "Then he said to Him, 'If Thy presence does not go with us, do not lead us up from here'" (Exodus 33:15). If God, even symbolically, did not accompany the Hebrew people on their trek to Canaan, then Moses did not want to move a step further. Considering that he was standing in the desert and Canaan was flowing with milk and honey, these words expressed loving dependence rather than defiance—and God knew it! Moses finished his soliloquy to his heavenly Father by noting that it was God's physical presence that distinguished Israel from the surrounding pagan nations.

Can we melt God's heart? Can we speak genuine words of love that give Him such pleasure that He appears to change His focus from one of justice to one of deep love and gracious generosity? We know that God is not a man that He should change His mind because of our eloquence. He is sovereign, all powerful, and unchanging in His perfection. But this desert scenario shows us that God derives great pleasure when we appeal to Him on the basis of our love relationship, rather than trying to convince Him of our innocence. He will not ignore sin—neither will He turn away from a human heart that humbly and genuinely wants to know Him more deeply.

How did God respond to Moses' decision to change the subject? We read, "And the Lord said to Moses, 'I will also do this thing of which you have spoken; for you have found favor in My sight, and I have known you by name'" (Exodus 33:17). These are the same issues that Moses brought up in verse 12 but in reverse order.

How amazing! The whole nation of Israel is literally standing in camp waiting to hear God's judgment on them for worshipping the golden calf. Moses is wholly focused on God and how much he wants to learn about Him and His ways. God appears to turn His attention away from this disobedient nation of Israel to this one man whose heart is devoted to Him.

What will be Moses' next response to God? He is so engulfed in God's beauty and majesty that he wants to see more! Moses says to God, "I pray Thee, show me Thy glory!" (Exodus 33:18). I get the feeling that we are looking in on a very private moment between Moses and his heavenly Father. Their relationship has grown for almost eighty years. Now Moses wants to see and experience more of the glory and beauty of God. You might think that God would say something to Moses like, "Moses, I appreciate the ardor of your love and your worship, but you really don't know what you are asking. Besides, the whole nation of Israel is waiting on Me here and so I really must attend to them."

Exodus 33:19-23 describes one of the greatest demonstrations of divine glory before an audience of *one* ever recorded in the history of mankind. In verse 19 God tells Moses, "I Myself will make all My goodness pass before you, and will proclaim the name of the Lord before you." At the same time, He announces His sovereignty which allows Him to exercise graciousness and compassion on those He chooses, solely on the basis of His own will. Always conscious of the physical needs of His children, God warns Moses that His glory is beyond anything that this former sheepherder from Midian could comprehend—furthermore, no human can gaze upon God's glorious presence.

Notice God's kindness as He prepares Moses for this unique experience: "Then the Lord said, 'Behold, there is a place *by Me*, and you shall stand there *on the rock*' [emphasis added]" (Verse 21). Two phrases stand out. First, God is saying that He wants Moses to stand next to Him—close by His side. Second, God tells him that he is to stand there on the rock. Jesus Christ is commonly referred to as a rock in Scripture. Once again, God is reminding Moses and the nation of Israel that Old Testament history is all about the Messiah, Jesus Christ, and Moses must be standing on *the rock* in order to please Him.

As far as we know from Scripture, God the Father is not confined to having literal hands, since He is an omnipresent spirit. But in tenderness, God says that He is going to place Moses in the *cleft of the rock*. Surely this rock is the one referred to earlier because anyone who is a true child of God is in Christ. For intimacy sake, God says He will cover Moses with His hand so that His glory would not destroy him. God finished His instructions with words that we can only understand in part. The God of Israel tells Moses that once He has passed by He will take away His hand so that

Moses will only see His back. God leaves us to ponder so many questions about His person, presence, and glory. What comes through very clearly, however, is God's profound love for the person who is devoted to Him. God has been focusing here on Moses, who wants to know Him more deeply. Is it too much to assume that this same God, who is unchanging, gives this same undivided attention to each of His worshipping children?

Before we leave this marvelous occasion that occurred in the barren Arabian Desert, let's look at some final exchanges between Moses and his God. You remember that God wasn't the only one who was angry at Israel's pagan worship of the calf. God had given Moses His Ten Commandments on two tablets of stone—Moses, in righteous anger, had destroyed the tablets. At the start of chapter 34, God tells Moses to prepare two more stone tablets because He still wants Israel to have His laws. Moses did what he was told. Early in the morning he climbed Mount Sinai with the new tablets to once again receive the Ten Commandments—a time spent between him and God alone. Can you picture the scene as verse 5 paints it? "And the Lord descended in the cloud and stood there with him as he called upon the name of the Lord." What an amazing relationship of friendship and love! Just imagine the joy in Moses' heart, as he stood next to the one true God who is without beginning and without end.

God then added to the list of His attributes of majesty, goodness, and sovereignty: "Then the Lord passed by in front of him and proclaimed, 'The Lord, the Lord God, compassionate and gracious, slow to anger, and abounding in lovingkindness and truth; who keeps lovingkindness for thousands, who forgives iniquity, transgression and sin; yet He will by no means leave the guilty unpunished'" (Exodus 34:6-7).

How does this description of God affect you? Does it not make you want to trust Him; to get to know Him more deeply; to learn even more of His attributes; and to observe how, in His timelessness, He enters our personal world in order to show us His love? How appropriate that the next verse deals with the worship of the only one who is truly worthy of it: "And Moses made haste to bow low toward the earth and worship" (Exodus 34:8). I can't imagine what Moses' nervous system was experiencing at that moment. After the apostle Peter watched the transfiguration of Jesus Christ, all he could think of doing was building three monuments to keep that special moment from dwindling into past history: "Lord, it is good for us to be here; if You wish, I will make three tabernacles here, one for You, and one for Moses, and one for Elijah" (Matthew 17:4). I don't suppose any earthly language is capable of describing exactly what Moses had experienced in the previous several days.

In order to keep on course with the subject of God's rest, we need to see the connection between the topic of running and this desert incident involving Moses. What does running have to do with resting and what does resting have to do with God's wonderful revelation of His glory to Moses? It will become clearer as we continue to read on through the New Testament. God's will for mankind from Eden forward, was that they experience a deep level of intimacy and communion with Him. This relationship of devotion with God is one of rest. Why is it so important to stress this topic? Many of those who have come to know Jesus Christ as their Savior do not routinely experience that rest. God doesn't force it on His children. Rather, He makes it available as a free gift to every believer. In the book of Hebrews, we read that God's rest is not something new, but has existed "from the foundation of the world" (Hebrews 4:3). Despite the fact that He has already prepared His rest for us, we often set about to live the Christian life as if its outcome depends on us.

One of the exciting things about God's rest is that it is not speaking of physical inactivity but an attitude of heart and spirit that can only be experienced by faith. The Christian life really is like participating in a race. The apostle Paul instructs us, "Do you not know that those who run in a race all run, but only one receives the prize? Run in such a way that you may win" (I Corinthians 9:24). Does this verse teach that we should lead highly competitive lives so that we will win instead of someone else? Not when we realize that God's will for His children is for them to enter into His rest. Notice that the last word of I Corinthians 9 is *disqualified*. Paul is not saying that you have to run the Christian life with an aggressively competitive attitude or you will lose your salvation. I believe it means that we will fall short of God's best—a life of divine intimacy that He has prepared for each one of us who trusts in His glorious Son.

Do you remember Galatians 5:7? "You were running well; who hindered you from obeying the truth?" Paul again speaks of running: "I press on toward the goal for the prize of the upward call of God in Christ Jesus" (Philippians 3:14). What prize is Paul talking about? Is he striving to receive more glory than the next person? No! Verse 10 says, "That I may know Him."

This goal of Paul's resonates with Moses' request in Exodus 33:13, "If I have found favor in Thy sight, let me know Thy ways, *that I may know Thee* [emphasis added]." They both wanted to know God intimately through entering into His rest. How thrilling when God responded to Moses' request, "And He said, 'My presence shall go with you, and I will give you rest'" (Exodus 33:14). Did God say something about rest? He certainly did! In response to Moses' request to know more about his heavenly Father and His ways, God promised that His very presence would be deeply and personally real to Moses, even while Moses led Israel on to Canaan.

May our dear Lord Jesus thrill you with the prospect of entering into His rest by faith, so that His very life becomes the only thing for which you long.

CHAPTER THREE – THEMES FOR FURTHER STUDY

- In both the Old and New Testaments, we discover that we must *stand on the rock* by faith (a symbolic reference to Jesus Christ) in order to please God the Father. (Exodus 33:21-22)

- Only Jesus Christ knows how to live the Christian life in a way that pleases the Father, and He is willing to live His divine life through us. (Matthew 3:17)

- If we refuse to depend on Christ to live the Christian life through us but insist on striving to please God by our own efforts, Jesus will not compete with us, but will step aside and wait until we turn to Him by faith. (Romans 7:14-25)

Chapter 4

BURNT OUT AND ON THE RUN

In my early teens, a western movie called *Shane*[1] captivated my young imagination. Shane, played by Alan Ladd, was the epitome of integrity even though he was a man with a mysterious past. One day he drifts into a western town and ends up working for a homesteading couple with an impressionable son, Joey. Before long, Shane is the young lad's hero.

As in a lot of western movies, this small town has a land baron whose greedy eyes are intent on increasing his wealth and power. To help him move the homesteaders off the range, he hires a professional gunslinger, played by Jack Palance—tall, mean, and dressed completely in black. Even if you never saw the movie, you can guess the last fifteen minutes. Shane, dressed in tan buckskin, is eventually pressured into a showdown with the man in black at the town saloon, and good overcomes evil once again. Because Shane has killed a man, he has to move on—much to the anguish of the young boy. As Shane rides out of town and off to who-knows-where, Joey's sad cry is repeated over and over, "Shane! Shane! Come back!"

This cowboy was my hero as well! I don't know if it's fair to compare one of God's prophets with a Hollywood gunfighter, but in the case of Elijah, there is a great deal of similarity. In I Kings chapter 18 we read about one of the most dramatic and miraculous showdowns between good and evil recorded anywhere in the Bible—complete with fire from heaven.

When Ahab, King of Israel, first comes to Elijah, he throws common courtesy to the wind and snarls, "Is this you, you troubler of Israel?" (I Kings 18:17). Elijah isn't intimidated at all—even by a king—but responds with a request, "Now then send and gather to me all Israel at Mount Carmel, together with 450 prophets of Baal and 400 prophets of the Asherah, who eat at Jezebel's table" (I Kings 18:19).

Elijah has never traveled this particular path before, but he still has the divinely inspired confidence that the God of Israel will vindicate His holy name.

It's difficult to read the next twenty verses without smiling. Not only does Elijah triumph in awesome fashion over the 850 prophets but his sarcasm, coupled with the ridiculous gyrations of the bogus prophets, make for a hilarious melodrama. It's such a bizarre scene that it's easy to visualize it in your imagination. You want to cheer out loud for Elijah.

Not one to gloat in victory, Elijah quickly turns to his heavenly Father in front of Israel and King Ahab's throng: "'Answer me, O Lord, answer me, that this people may know that Thou, O Lord, art God, and that Thou hast turned their heart back again.' Then the fire of the Lord fell, and consumed the burnt offering and the wood and the stones and the dust, and licked up the water that was in the trench. And when all the people saw it, they fell on their faces; and they said, 'The Lord, He is God; the Lord, He is God'" (I Kings 18:37-39).

There are many lessons for us in this exciting chapter. Once the smoke clears away from the contest site on Mount Carmel, it's obvious who really is "the God who answers by fire." Elijah reprimands Israel, "'How long will you hesitate between two opinions? If the Lord is God, follow Him; but if Baal, follow him.' But the people did not answer him a word" (I Kings 18:21). The bite in this verse is a universal question that is equally applicable today as then.

The saga of Elijah's victory over the prophets of Baal is the threshold of a total character change in the mighty prophet Elijah. It's hard to conceive that the timid man we are about to meet in chapter 19 is the same bold mouthpiece for God who not only called down fire from heaven but subsequently killed all the prophets of Baal. We can probably identify more with the timid Elijah than with the brash one.

Let's meet this new Elijah, now that the contest is over and good has triumphed over evil.

FINDING PEACE IN THE FACE OF THREATS

When Queen Jezebel learns that Elijah has killed all of her hireling prophets of Baal, she doesn't spend any time wringing her hands. Her response is swift and deadly. She immediately sends a messenger to the prophet with this death threat: "So may the gods do to me and even more, if I do not make your life as the life of one of them by tomorrow about this time" (I Kings 19:2). You have to at least give Jezebel credit for being a clear communicator.

Once Elijah hears that the queen has put a twenty-four hour bounty on his head, he seems to fall apart emotionally. All he can think about is *escape*. We don't want to minimize the seriousness of the situation, because Jezebel could certainly make good on her threat. However, there is much that we can learn about human nature and especially about the character of God by closely examining this chapter.

Almost as soon as Elijah reads the message from King Ahab's conniving wife, we are told, "And he was afraid and arose and ran for his life and came to Beersheba" (I Kings 19:3). You and I will probably never face a threat of this magnitude. Maybe our threats will come from:

1. Our neighbor – "If your dog keeps coming over and digging in my yard, I'm going to sue you," or
2. Our employer – "Unless you are prepared to invest sixty plus hours per week in this company, you are going to have to look for another job," or,
3. Our banker – "If your monthly car loan payment does not reach us by the due date, we can legally seize your car."

WHEN RUNNING AWAY SEEMS LIKE THE ONLY OPTION

My purpose is not to stand in judgment on Elijah. I just can't help asking, "What has changed?" One fact stands out rather vividly. Elijah failed to immediately turn to God in dependent prayer and trust Him as he had done many times in the past.

Our heavenly Father allows crises to invade our lives for basically the same reason—to teach us to depend on Him so that we are helped and He is glorified. What if we fail to turn to Him right away in faith when we are bombarded by trials? Sometimes God provides and protects anyway—simply by His grace. But how He longs to have us draw upon His Father-love. Nowhere is this more clearly stated than in Proverbs: "Trust in the Lord with all your heart, and do not lean on your own understanding. In all your ways acknowledge Him, and He will make your paths straight" (Proverbs 3:5-6).

Jezebel's threat pierces deeply into Elijah's soul. Every thought of God's help is squeezed out by imagining all the torture methods at the queen's disposal. The one thought that Elijah does entertain is this—run for your life! So he and his servant run to Beersheba, a little more than a hundred miles away.

Our choices tend to be like links of a chain—a wrong decision can result in a whole sequence of wrong choices. Very few of us ever have to literally run for our lives but we all have our *Jezebel moments* when everything around us seems on the verge of collapse. Is our next step to lay the situation before the Lord in prayer, or is it to stumble into a string of wrong decisions?

I see the same inconsistency in my own life when a crisis comes along. At times when I am first confronted with danger, I choose to share it with the Lord. He not only works out the situation for my growth and His glory, but He also fortifies my spirit with His peaceful rest. All too often, however, at the same bulls-eye of a crisis, my mind shifts into self-control. With no thought of leaning on the Lord, I run down lists of personal solutions in my mind, drawn from previous experience.

TRUSTING OTHERS WHEN WE NEED THEM THE MOST

Almost missed at the end of verse 3 of the nineteenth chapter is the small phrase, "and left his servant there." What a serious mistake Elijah was making by not allowing his servant to be there with him when he was emotionally exhausted and vulnerable.

One of the biggest problems with choosing to depend on our own skill and experience is that the Holy Spirit can no longer focus all the wisdom of God toward resolving our problems. Elijah started his day by choosing to run away from Jezebel and her deadly threat—things seem to have spiraled downhill from there. He arrived safely at Beersheba, but he made another questionable choice—he left his servant and companion there. Elijah may have felt like he wanted to be alone but what he really needed at that moment was the input of someone who was sensitive to the Lord.

The prophet is running scared as he enters Beersheba. His servant could undoubtedly have given more objective insight into the prophet's best choices, such as, "Why don't we take a little time to stop and pray?" Elijah sees his trusted servant as a liability so he dismisses him. How unfortunate for both men!

The apostle Paul writes, "But God has so composed the body, giving more abundant honor to that member which lacked, that there should be no division in the body, but that the members should have the same care for one another" (I Corinthians 12:24-25). God has made it clear in Scripture that He desires believers to be primarily dependent on Him. However, it pleases Him when Christians also look to other members of His body for counsel. For this mutual care to happen, we have to keep the walls from forming around us, and give others the freedom to enter into our lives. Elijah cut himself off from the counsel and encouragement of his servant when the prophet left his friend at Beersheba and headed into the wilderness alone.

WHY DO WE PICK THE WILDERNESS WHEN WE PANIC?

"But he himself went a day's journey into the wilderness, and came and sat down under a juniper tree; and he requested for himself that he might die" (I Kings 19:4).

At this point of the story, we still have no indication that Elijah has consulted with God. As he shades himself under the juniper tree he must be thinking to himself, "How did I ever get from Mount Carmel to this miserable place?" That's exactly how life looks when we fail to enter God's rest—hot, dry, and lifeless.

Isn't it interesting that when we choose to work through a crisis in our own strength and avoid turning to God, we invariably follow a similar downward spiral?

1. We experience emotions such as fear, anger, and anxiety.
2. We try to run from the irritation.
3. We isolate ourselves from the objective counsel of others.
4. We run deeper into the wilderness by making a series of wrong choices.
5. We decide, in our own negative frame of mind, that we cannot possibly suffer any more. We've reached our limit.
6. We become overwhelmed with depression.
7. The only reasonable and available choice seems to be death.

You and I often find ourselves *in the wilderness* in our daily Christian lives, and the thing that is hard to reckon with is that we *choose* to be there. I am not minimizing the pain of the traumatic scenarios that God often permits in our lives. But the Lord Jesus has made His own life available to us for those times. He urges us in Scripture to connect to Him by faith—or as John 15 states it, to *abide in Christ*, just like a branch abides in a vine. He doesn't even promise that the trauma won't be excruciatingly painful. He simply says that He will carry the weight of the ordeal on His sufficient shoulders and will pour His blessed life into ours. The alternative to resting in Him is the wilderness. When Elijah was threatened with death, he chose the parched desert of self-sufficiency over the still waters of God's rest.

CHOOSING DEATH OVER FELLOWSHIP WITH GOD

Have you noticed that when stresses begin to pound us like unrelenting waves beating on the shore, we tend to think of only two choices? One choice is to bring all of our own personal strength and experience to bear upon the crisis and try to mitigate the damage. The other choice, in our imaginations at least, is to fly away like a bird from our bodies and our pressure-filled lives, so these frustrations can never bother us again.

If we were to ask the Lord which of these two choices He would prefer for us, I'm sure He would say, "Neither one!" According to verse 4, Elijah started with the first choice—his own wisdom—and now he is inquiring of God regarding the second—asking his heavenly Father to snuff out his life. Elijah's exact words reveal a man who is convinced he cannot bear any more stress. So he concludes, "It is enough; now, O Lord, take my life, for I am not better than my fathers" (I Kings 19:4).

The intention of this study is not to minimize the reality of what Elijah experienced or what devastating situation you and I might face. There was a time when the accumulated pressure of my work almost swept me away. At the moment when we feel hemmed in and none of our choices seem to offer us any hope, we may think we have to solve our own problems.

That is where we need to learn to rest in God. He loves His children with an infinite love and His omniscience allows Him to know whether to take us through a trial to teach us dependence on Him, or to tenderly nurture us so we will be encouraged. In some cases, God's children give up on self during catastrophic times and turn to their Father. In other cases they just give up.

If there had been a counselor or therapist in the desert with the prophet, I can picture them saying, "Elijah, in my professional opinion, you are experiencing *burnout*." Even though this term is synonymous with the "information generation" of today, Elijah seemed to demonstrate all the classic symptoms approximately three thousand years ago.

Carrie Sydnor Coffman, a missionary who experienced burnout herself, interviewed a number of her colleagues suffering with the same condition and gained some valuable insights. She writes, "There are times when God does ask us to put out an extreme effort. But on a daily basis, God is far more reasonable than His driven servants seem to think. We give the impression that God is a cruel taskmaster, not the giver of abundant life."[2]

Another conclusion Carrie came to is, "God is a relational God. He made us in His image. Thus, relationship, not getting things done, is primary. Often people who burn out are in a constant hurry to get more things done. Ministry becomes the all-consuming focus. Frequently they don't take time for emotionally satisfying relationships."[3]

What is burnout? Christina Maslach gives one of the clearest definitions: "Burnout is a syndrome of emotional exhaustion, depersonalization, and reduced personal accomplishment that can occur among individuals who do 'people-work' of some kind. It is a response to the chronic emotional strain of dealing extensively with other human beings, particularly when they are troubled or having problems."[4]

Let's review Elijah's condition in the light of this definition:

1. EMOTIONAL EXHAUSTION – "PEOPLE FEEL DRAINED AND USED UP. THEY LACK ENOUGH ENERGY TO FACE ANOTHER DAY. THEIR EMOTIONAL RESOURCES ARE DEPLETED..."

In I Kings chapter 19 we read that while Elijah is sitting under the juniper tree, drowning in self-pity, he lies down and falls into an exhausted sleep. One difficulty with sleeping in the midst of burnout is that the sufferers feel like they require more of it, since they are in a constant state of weariness. Regardless of how long they sleep, they still wake up exhausted and weak.

It's important to realize that there is a difference between *stress* and *burnout*. Stress is a part of everyday life and can be caused by situations as benign as giving your opinion at a PTA meeting or getting an unexpected bill in the mail. Burnout, on the other hand, is caused by unrelenting stress. Stressed people can see themselves getting on top of their workload with more time. Burned out people don't care one way or another.

From the Biblical narrative it seems like Elijah has reached the point of burnout. He doesn't have the emotional energy to face the crisis involving Queen Jezebel and her death threat. He has reached the "enough" point, and the only logical choice, as he runs it through his negative grid, is death.

2. REDUCED PERSONAL ACCOMPLISHMENT – "A GNAWING SENSE OF INADEQUACY ABOUT THEIR ABILITY TO RELATE TO RECIPIENTS. THIS MAY RESULT IN A SELF-IMPOSED VERDICT OF FAILURE."

The scary part of burnout is that the mind is so mired in an absence of hope that there doesn't seem to be any good reason to look for a solution to the problem. Elijah has obviously given up—even the possibility of asking the Lord for strength and courage to face this vengeful queen is too overwhelming. The thought of being an instrument in God's hand to deal with this wicked royal family doesn't seem to even enter the prophet's mind.

What a contrast with the Psalmist who wrote in his time of personal crisis, "Rescue me, O my God, out of the hand of the wicked, out of the grasp of the wrongdoer and ruthless man, for Thou art my hope; O Lord God, Thou art my confidence from my youth" (Psalm 71:4-5).

We twenty-first century Christians have an advantage that Elijah did not have—the entire divinely inspired Word of God. What a source of hope Scripture is! Hope is one of a long list of benefits that are ours when we enter God's rest. But hope is a person, not a thing. Colossians 1:27 says, "Christ in you, the hope of glory." In fact, the entire trinity of the Godhead is involved in promoting hope in the Christian's heart, "Now may the God of hope fill you with all joy and peace in believing, that you may abound in hope by the power of the Holy Spirit" (Romans 15:13).

3. DEPERSONALIZATION – "THE DEVELOPMENT OF THIS DETACHED, CALLOUS, AND EVEN DEHUMANIZED RESPONSE..."

One verse in this story clearly demonstrates the negative attitude toward other people that is so characteristic of burnout. When God eventually asks, "What are you doing here, Elijah?" the prophet launches into a dialogue which seems to paint Israel in dark colors and himself in bright hues. Elijah complained, "I have been very zealous for the Lord, the God of hosts; for the sons of Israel have forsaken Thy covenant, torn down Thine altars and killed Thy prophets with the sword. And I alone am left; and they seek my life, to take it away" (I Kings 19:10).

Someone has wisely pointed out that when we look at Jesus' few comments while He hung on Calvary's cross, it is clear that our complaining attitudes do not spring from His pure heart. Picture the scenario. The Lord Jesus was experiencing excruciating pain from the cuts on top of His head, the raw skin of His face, the shredding of His back muscles, the bruising of His torso, arms, and legs, and the piercing of His hands and feet. From a human standpoint Jesus had every right to criticize the Pharisees for their blindness;

the high priest for his arrogance; Pilate and Herod for their weakness; Peter for his denial; all of His disciples for their desertion; the Roman Empire for its cruelty; and the whole nation of Israel for its stubborn disobedience. At this historical moment, I'm sure the Son of God chose His words carefully. The following, according to the Gospels' record, is the sum total of His words as He hung on the cross, wracked with pain:

- "Father, forgive them; for they do not know what they are doing" (Luke 23:34).
- "Truly I say to you, today you shall be with Me in Paradise" (Luke 23:43).
- "Woman, behold, your son!" and, "Behold, your mother!" (John 19:26-27).
- "I am thirsty" (John 19:28).
- "My God, My God, why hast Thou forsaken Me?" (Matthew 27:46).
- "Father, into Thy hands I commit My spirit" (Luke 23:46).
- "It is finished!" (John 19:30).

The Bible makes it vividly clear that Elijah is a courageous man of God who refuses to be intimidated by kings and pagan priests. However, in this situation involving Jezebel's threat he neglects to turn to His God—the Shepherd of Israel—and allow Him to deal with this wicked woman. As a result, Elijah fails to enter into God's rest and experience the consequences.

When we consider Christ's gracious words from the Cross, we are tempted to say, "Yes, but He is God—what else would you expect?" However, we must remember that another benefit of entering God's rest is the access this grants us to the mind of Christ. Savor this verse from *The Amplified Bible* that the apostle Paul wrote to the Corinthian Christians and see if it doesn't bring rest to your heart: "But we have the mind of Christ (the Messiah) and do hold the thoughts (feelings and purposes) of His heart" (I Corinthians 2:16).[5]

Isn't that truth almost unbelievable? When Christians turn to the Lord by faith as the solution to a threatening crisis, God's Word states that our minds become conduits for Christ's thoughts and feelings. He gives us help and direction at the very point of need. I don't know about you, but I'm certain that's the kind of help I want when I am about to be overwhelmed!

CHAPTER FOUR – THEMES FOR FURTHER STUDY

- Following Elijah's successful contest with the prophets of Baal, he gives a very simple piece of advice: "How long will you hesitate between two opinions? If the Lord is God, follow Him; but if Baal, follow him." List some specific examples of how we could apply that wise counsel to our own daily lives as Christians. (I Timothy 6:11-14)

- When Elijah received the news of Jezebel's threat he had at least two choices. He could share it with his heavenly Father and wait for His direction, or he could deal with the danger by his own instincts and experience. We have the very same two choices in the face of a crisis. (Philippians 4: 13, 19)

- We can literally run away from trouble with our feet or by avoidance, denial, and plain disobedience. Has God ever urged you to talk frankly to someone about an important matter and you chose not to? (Galatians 6:1-2)

- As Christians, we have the wonderful privilege of being members of a spiritual body. Our Father gives each of His children a variety of spiritual gifts so that we can help and build up each other—even in the very worst situations. (I Corinthians, chapters 12 and 13)

- It's pretty clear from Scripture that Elijah was drowning in self pity. What issues do you think lie at the bottom of this character quality? Can you recognize it in yourself? (I Samuel 15:10-35)

- A major difference between stress and burnout is that in the latter case there is an absence of *hope*. (I Peter 1:3)

- Often, Christians accept *complaining* as a personal right. We only have to look at Jesus Christ nailed to the wooden cross and His few constructive comments, to realize that a complaining spirit does not originate from Him. (Isaiah 53:2-7)

Chapter 5

THE SAGA OF THE OBNOXIOUS OX

Whenever I hear the word *yoke*, a wonderful story comes to my mind that a missionary on furlough from Bolivia, South America, related many years ago. He had ridden in an oxcart owned by a Bolivian national man. The pair of oxen was fastened together by a wooden yoke, but that's where the similarity between the two animals ended! On the right side of the yoke was a large female ox that had obviously pulled this cart for many years. She was accustomed to the yoke—steady, consistent, and focused. But it's the ox on the left with which I can identify. That ox was a young bull in training. He did not want to be in the yoke so he was doing everything possible to get out of it. I picture him lunging forward; trying to lie down; stiffening his legs; going straight up and trying to leap sideways. This young bull was all testosterone and no common sense. He was determined to make it difficult for everyone else and he was beating himself to death trying to accomplish that task. Instead of pulling any part of the load, he was probably adding to his partner's work. He was in training, but fighting it aggressively all the way down the road.

As obnoxious as the young bull was, the mature ox was the definition of steadiness. It would be interesting to know how many young trainees she had schooled in the past. She obviously was not seriously affected by her partner's lack of cooperation. She just kept pulling the cart straight ahead, guided only by her owner's wishes.

There are so many great lessons in this story, but first I want to focus on several of my favorite Bible verses that bring me such comfort. They say, "Come to Me, all who are weary and heavy-laden, and I will give you rest. Take My yoke upon you, and learn from Me, for I am gentle and humble in heart; and you shall find rest for your souls. For My yoke is easy, and My load is light" (Matthew 11:28-30). Certainly one could meditate on this treasure of truth for a lifetime and still find new truths.

VERSE 28:
- COME – What a friendly word of invitation! Does it conjure up in your mind a picture of Jesus Christ, with nail pierced hands outstretched and the kindest smile of assurance on His face? I can almost hear Him saying, "Do not be afraid," just like He did in Matthew 28:10 when He appeared to some of the disciples following His resurrection from the grave. How sensitive of Him to be conscious of our fears and want to set our hearts at ease. In the immediate context of Matthew 11, Jesus is talking to those gathered around Him who can literally hear His voice. In another sense, He is reaching out to the entire world, saying, "It doesn't matter what your language is; it doesn't matter if you have a pig tusk through your nose and still use bows and arrows; it doesn't even matter whether you are a Wall Street power broker; just come to Me!" Jesus' petition is addressed to those who are believers in Him as well as to those

who thus far have wanted nothing to do with Him. He urges both groups to come to Him, even though the motives and the reward for coming are poles apart. And that is part of the beauty and grace in Christ's simple invitation to all mankind, "Come!"

- TO ME – It is so important that we catch this short little phrase and not pass right over it because in it is the way to eternal life. To miss it can mean that one can lead a long life and not understand fully the *why* of life. The primary reason for coming to Jesus is because we are lost, helpless, hopeless, and without a spiritual leg to stand on. We are invited to come to a *person*, not an ideology or a philosophy. That same Jesus is currently in heaven with God the Father: "If then you have been raised up with Christ, keep seeking the things above, where Christ is, seated at the right hand of God" (Colossians 3:1). His promise is as good today as it was two thousand years ago when He first proclaimed it. And He says, "Come to Me!"

But what if I am full of pride, selfishness, and greed? Jesus seems to be saying, "Come to Me and believe that I died on that old rugged cross to pay the sin debt that you couldn't pay yourself. I took your place! But you must come to Me to be totally forgiven." You may say, "But I have been a good person, a loyal husband and father. I provided for my family and even sacrificed for them. I can't think of a single law that I've broken, other than maybe driving over the speed limit a few times." Jesus could reply, "I wrote in my Word that the totality of a person's supposed good works is like a pile of filthy rags that you wouldn't even consider touching: 'For all of us have become like one who is unclean, and all our righteous deeds are like a filthy garment' (Isaiah 64:6). That is why I say, 'Come to Me! Leave those filthy rags in the past; believe in My death for you. You can't offer Me anything sufficiently worthwhile that you have done to save yourself. I can offer you eternal life in heaven. Just come to Me!'"

What if I am already a Christian and yet I find life just as crazy? It seems like the harder I try to live a victorious life, the farther behind I fall. Maybe I have been a believer for thirty years and yet I am still thinking many of the same kind of immoral thoughts that I did before. I still get angry. I bend the truth to suit my situation and I don't seem to be able to get along with my fellow workers. I don't see what is so victorious about the Christian life. Maybe I'm not even a believer after all. Jesus could be saying, "You can't grow and mature spiritually by all your striving and exertion, any more than you can gain forgiveness of sin and eternal life by the same means. Come to Me by faith! Just as I provided salvation, I am providing the joyous Christian life. I came by the Holy Spirit's power, to live inside you when you believed in Me. Only I can live the Christian life—you don't even know where to begin. I have the power and ability to live the one life that your heavenly Father wants to see in you—my life! I will not compete with you. If you insist on doing it yourself, I will stand to the side and let you, because that's My nature. It's not because I am mean—it's just that you will not come to Me and Me alone until you get tired of your own failures. So why don't you come to Me and I will live the Christian life through you?"

- ALL – Don't you love this word? If our heavenly Father only allowed certain personality types, ethnic groups, or education levels to come to Him, then I would nervously have to pore over the list to make sure that I was on it. If the verse used the term *most*, there would still be a chance that I would be counted among the small group who are not allowed to come.

What if I found that something about me, disqualified me from coming? Then I would have to stop reading all that came after because it did not apply to me. But when I read the word *all*, I can rest—I even get a smile on my face. It might as well say, "You there! Bryan! I want you to come to me every bit as much as I want anyone else. Everything that I make available to them, I will make available to you too."

- WEARY – Is *weary* the only requirement to be numbered among the *all*? At times I have been weary and discouraged. In fact, there was a time that I came so close to a burnout that I felt like I could see it in the distance. It's as if Jesus says, "That's right! That's what I mean by 'weary.' That qualifies you. Why don't you come to Me?" Even as I write this, thankfulness wells up in my heart to God who says that there is *no one* who has sinned so much or failed so much that they no longer qualify to come.

It's interesting that God in His infinite wisdom doesn't have to give a list of details so we can determine if our particular weariness qualifies; like an IRS tax bulletin. And that's the beautiful thing about Jesus Christ. As John 3:16 so wonderfully expresses, God loves the whole world and so He generously invites *everyone*—all who are weary—to come to Him.

- AND HEAVY-LADEN – This expression has the meaning of loading something down or filling something up to the extent that it is almost at the danger point. We have all seen pictures of a donkey in the Middle East piled high with a variety of objects. I recently saw a photo taken somewhere in Asia of a family of five on a motorcycle. That is *heavy-laden*! The phrase can also refer to spiritual anxiety, which would qualify it as an oxymoron. *Spiritual* and *anxiety* are not normally used together. Half of the Lord's invitation to come to Him is directed at those who are *heavy-laden,* or, in other words, spiritually anxious. Are there really that many Christians who are not experiencing God's rest? Of all people, Jesus would know, wouldn't He? Jesus simply invited those who were weary or spiritually anxious in the group of people He was with to come to Him for help.

Our family attends a church that has several thousand participants. I often look across row after row of faces, all directed toward the platform, and wonder how many in this huge group are true Christians, are suffering from cancer, are having an affair, or are contemplating suicide. Are there those who have given up trying to live a victorious Christian life because of their string of dreadful failures since they first trusted in Christ? We all look so scrubbed there in church but how many are like the picture of that little donkey—weary and overloaded?

- AND I [Jesus] – Where do you begin with this wonderful promise? Think for a moment of the various religions around the world. There are at least two common factors in all of them. One factor is that these religions are all very complicated so the average adherent can only give the briefest of descriptions when asked, "What is the spiritual foundation of your religion?" The second factor is that almost all require one to do good deeds to some impossible level, so that they can never be sure of achieving eternal life with God. If an adult who practices a religion can't explain it, how in the world could a child understand? That is one of the beautiful things about Biblical Christianity. A young child can understand the Bible's explanation of salvation. What is that profound truth that even little children are capable of understanding? In its simplest form, Jesus says to people of all ages from all countries, "Come to Me! If you are a sinner on the way to hell, come to Me. Believe in your heart that I died on the cross to pay for your sin—I took the place that you deserve. After three days in the grave, I miraculously arose and returned to heaven to be with God the Father. I did that because I love you. I did it all—you just have to believe Me." Yes, a small child can understand that!

When my son Dan was five years old, he heard the teacher in his Bible class explain the same Gospel. That afternoon he was outside playing in a snow fort and his young heart responded in faith to that simple Bible truth—that Jesus, who is perfect, died in his place and paid for his sin. He believed it and in his five-year-old way, he thanked Jesus for doing that. Thirty years later, it thrills me to see Dan explaining these same Biblical truths to his five-year-old son (my grandson).

I believe that when Jesus addressed the weary and heavy-laden that day, He was also speaking to those who were genuine Christians. They had believed in Him as their Messiah and by faith were trusting in His future sacrifice for them. But whereas their new lives in Him ought to have been filled with Christ's love, joy, peace, and patience, they were still weary and spiritually anxious. The invitation was the same, "Come to Me!" They didn't have to strive to attain or jump through any hoops. By faith they only had to enter into His rest.

- WILL GIVE YOU – This amazing verse 28 is full of simple little words that we probably say many times each day. That is likely why we miss the depth of the meaning. The blessedness of this phrase is the little word "give." So many of the religions of the world are symbolized by verbs like: *offer, donate, try, deny, do without, pay, and improve.* And it all takes place in the same direction—from the adherent toward the deity or system.

I have had the privilege of visiting the country of Thailand several times. There are elaborate Buddhist temples in both the large cities and the small rural towns. If you look closely in restaurants and businesses, you can often see a plate of food, gifts, and flowers in front of a small statue of Buddha. Those offerings speak volumes about terms like *worthiness* and *merit*. Christianity doesn't use such terms unless they refer to the Lord Jesus Himself. Unlike the other religions of the world, Jesus is the divine giver and we are on the receiving end of it all. When we boil this down to its lowest common denominator, *religion* is all about mankind giving to their god because they have to, while *Christianity* is all about Jesus giving to mankind because He loves to.

I find it interesting how the topic of worthiness comes up in the story of the prodigal son in Luke 15. When the wayward son repents of his backslidden way of life and returns to his father, the son said, "Father, I have sinned against heaven and in your sight; *I am no longer worthy* to be called your son [emphasis added]" (Luke 15:21). The son has it wrong and the father picks up on it. He said that he was "no longer worthy" implying that he had been worthy before he left home. Notice that the father totally ignores the subject of worthiness. The story of the prodigal could be a picture of the repentant sinner coming to the Savior for salvation, but it's more likely a picture of the child of God who falls into sin and upon repenting returns to the fellowship of his Father and his family. Worthiness plays no part in either scenario. Likewise, the Lord Jesus doesn't talk about *worthiness* because none of us is worthy of either eternal salvation or fellowship with God. He freely gives us Himself. In response, we can only stand back in awe and sincere praise, and say, "Thank you, dear Jesus! I'm coming to You now by faith."

- REST – God's rest is like an opal. Have you ever seen an Australian opal with fire in it? It's beautiful! It generates a constantly changing spectrum of color against a milky white background. More expensive opals have what appears to be a burst of flame deep in the gem that seems to change shape as you move it. God's rest for His beloved children is like that—deep, intricate, and yet simple and beautiful to behold. Although we move into new levels of understanding as we grow into Christ's likeness, His rest remains simple and comfortable. Jesus concludes His statement by offering His rest to those who come to Him. Can you think of anyone who doesn't need a God designed rest?

In Luke 10, verses 38-42, we have a moving story that pictures what God's rest is and also what His rest is not. Jesus is visiting the home of His friends in Bethany—Mary, Martha, and their brother Lazarus. Martha is hospitality personified and seems to thrive when putting on a perfect dining experience. If she lived in the twenty-first century, she would probably greatly enjoy another Martha. All the while she is putting the final touches on the meal and the house, Mary is seated on the floor, mesmerized by the words of Jesus. God's Word describes Martha as being *distracted* with all her preparations. Another way of saying it would be that she is not experiencing God's rest. Would it be unfair to say of Martha that she has her priorities wrong? Mary is feeding on the words of the Savior—Martha wants to make sure that everything concerning the meal is just right. Mary doesn't care if they ever eat as long as she can continue to commune with Jesus. Martha is probably hoping that Jesus will rave about her outstanding hospitality.

We can almost hear Martha clearing her throat and sighing with emotions that seem to say to Mary, "Will you please get up off the floor and help me get the food on the table!" She apparently goes over the top when she says to Jesus, the creator of the universe, "Lord, do You not care that my sister has left me to do all the serving alone? Then tell her to help me" (Luke 10:40). Wow! We can all be blind to reality when we stop resting spiritually and allow our petty little grievances to take priority in our lives. Blind to everything but the tiny world of *me,* Martha is so angry that she challenges Jesus about whether He is caring or not. But it doesn't end there. She then *orders* Jesus, whose creative words spoke the galaxies into existence, to follow her bidding. I love what Jesus says and does at that very emotional moment. What He does *not* do is humiliate Martha for her comments and attitude but He lovingly reaches out and teaches her about the divine gift of His rest. Martha is most likely angry, hurt, and very brittle. The wrong response from Jesus could produce enormous hurt in her heart and possibly even a lifelong breech in their friendship. But Jesus, always the consummate speaker of truth in kindness, sums up all that He has witnessed for the past hour (totally ignoring the matter of food) by saying in the kindest way, "Martha, Martha, you are *worried* and *bothered* about *so many things* [emphasis added]" (Luke 10:41).

Hmm! "Worried" and "bothered" sound an awful lot like "weary" and "heavy laden", from Matthew 11. And what is the remedy for that? Jesus states in the Matthew account, "Come to Me!" and that's what Mary is doing. Jesus discerns that there are *so many things* about which Martha is upset. But rather than lecture her He highlights the wonderful truth that God's rest is not about *us.* It is all about Jesus! I love the way the New American Standard Version words it—Jesus says to Martha, "But only a few things are necessary." Then Jesus seems to correct Himself to be more specific, "really only *one*." What do you suppose the *one thing* is that encompasses their entire visit? It appears to be exactly what Mary is doing. She determined that while Jesus was in their house, she was going to bask in His presence and learn from Him. They could always eat just before Jesus retires for the night but while He is there, she only wants to dwell in His presence and enjoy His rest. Jesus concludes His point by saying, "Mary has chosen the *good* part, which shall not be taken away from her [emphasis added] (Luke 10:42). But Martha, dear Martha, chooses to be weary and heavy-laden!

CHAPTER FIVE – THEMES FOR FURTHER STUDY

- Jesus invites *all* who are weary to come to Him. No one is disqualified from coming—either for salvation or for forgiveness as a rebellious child of God. (Matthew 11:28)

- *Religion* is all about mankind giving to their deity because they *have to*—*Christianity* is all about Jesus giving to mankind because He *loves* to. (2 Corinthians 5:14-21)

- The terms *worthiness* and *merit* do not pertain to mankind, but only to the Godhead. (Revelation 5:11-14)

- When Christians come to Jesus Christ by faith, He responds by providing them with His spiritual rest. (Matthew 11:28-29)

Chapter 6

HOW CAN A YOKE BE COMFORTABLE?

The last time we pictured the young bull in the yoke with the mature ox he was charging in every direction except straight ahead. What a knucklehead! I don't know about you but I can see myself in that young trainee in so many different ways, thinking that activity alone will get something accomplished. But along the way, we begin to realize that all of our resistance at the thought of being yoked is only creating a lot of chafing and bruises.

During Jesus' three years of ministry on earth, He always chose meaningful illustrations to which His hearers could immediately relate. The stories were a part of their own culture. I'm sure the people of Judea regularly saw teams of oxen pulling carts of people and produce, yoked together for maximum ox power.

We looked closely at Matthew 11:28 in the previous chapter. Now, let's examine verses 29 and 30.

TAKE MY YOKE UPON YOU AND LEARN FROM ME

Whenever we hear the word *yoke* used, our imaginations picture two beasts of burden attached at their necks by a sturdy wooden brace. A secondary meaning of yoking two domestic animals together would be *submission*. Do you find that thought offensive? Does it cause you to recoil and say, "I don't want any part of a process where I lose my identity and become a robot, totally controlled by God"? In most cases a pair of oxen are equals fastened together in order to focus all their strength in one direction. However, Jesus' perspective is different. He does not expect us to be His equal in yoke bearing. And what a relief that is! Jesus is willing to link up with the believer who is weak, prone to wander, and uncertain of the road ahead. The marvel of this union is that we are invited into the yoke of one who is infinitely holy, all powerful, and eternal. It is so much better to be yoked together with someone who is perfect, rather than one with a list of weaknesses like our own.

It's easy to miss the little word *take* here in Matthew 11:29. It signals a choice that the Lord Jesus is giving us—a choice to link our daily lives with Him or not. Just as with salvation, God does not force a decision on us. He makes the provision and then with a generous heart full of love, He invites us to come. Jesus seems to be saying to the believer, "Only I know how to live the Christian life in a way that will please the Father, and I will do it by means of the Holy Spirit who dwells within you. If you try and work out the Christian life on your own, you will fail. Instead of experiencing the joy and fulfillment of the Spirit-controlled life, you will wrestle with frustration and failure. I will not *make* you join Me in the yoke, but if you do, I will carry the entire load. I will do all the pulling while you walk beside Me. You can experience My rest, but it is your choice."

As previously mentioned, in the meaning of the word yoke there is an element of *submission*. However, in this case it is toward a loving, generous Savior who demonstrated His love for us by standing silently before vile Roman soldiers while they spat their contempt in His dear face. He might say, "Not only have I provided everything you need to have your sins forgiven and receive eternal life, but now that you are My child, I am offering you a place in My yoke with Me. You don't have to. You will still be Mine if you don't. But I am telling you that this is the path to contentment, spiritual growth, and rest." If that's submission, when can I start?

As in the earlier illustration, the young bull ox did not need to know where his partner ox, the cart, the owner, and he were headed or the condition of the road ahead. The owner knew and that was enough. He would give direction all along the way. The young bull needed only to rest in the yoke, trusting in the owner's ability. What a wonderful picture of the Lord Jesus' provision for us to live the Christian life! Why then do we hesitate to enter into this yoke relationship with Him? Is it fear? Of what? Losing control of our lives? A deep distrust of how and where the Lord might lead us? So we continue on down the road of life resisting, balking at everything, and rarely resting in the satisfying love of Jesus Christ. Isn't that a strange paradox? The Lord is inviting us into a deep and intimate love relationship with Him but we are suspicious of it. We like the idea of being saved from hell but balk at submitting our will to that of our loving heavenly Father.

Jesus also tells us that if we willingly join Him in the yoke, we will experience a time of learning. Does that make you nervous? Do you wonder if He is planning hard lessons intended to soften you up for heaven? I think the learning has more to do with Jesus Christ teaching His fellow yoke-bearers new aspects about Himself, like He did with Moses. In response to Moses' request, "If I have found favor in Thy sight, let me know Thy ways, that I may know Thee" (Exodus 33:13), God was so pleased that He promised to go with him and the people of Israel into Canaan and also to bring them into His rest. This yoking with Jesus Christ, as the Bible calls God's rest, is not a *place* but a *relationship* with Jesus, whereby He teaches us more about Himself. The apostle Paul confirms this by saying, "More than that, I count all things to be loss in view of the surpassing value of *knowing Christ Jesus my Lord* [emphasis added]" *(*Philippians 3:8). And in verse 10, Paul declares, "That I may *know* Him [emphasis added]."

FOR I AM GENTLE AND HUMBLE IN HEART

Of all of Jesus' attributes He could mention here, He chooses two that we would not expect Him to highlight— *gentle* and *humble*. In the Psalms we read, "Who is the King of glory? The Lord strong and mighty, the Lord mighty in battle" (Psalm 24:8). Is this the same person who describes Himself as gentle and humble in heart? And again we read, "The voice of the Lord is powerful, the voice of the Lord is majestic. The voice of the Lord breaks the cedars; yes, the Lord breaks in pieces the cedars of Lebanon. And He makes Lebanon skip like a calf, and Sirion like a young wild ox. The voice of the Lord hews out flames of fire. The voice of the Lord shakes the wilderness; the Lord shakes the wilderness of Kadesh" (Psalm 29:4-8). Could this be the same Lord who tells us to come to Him because He is gentle and humble in heart?

Since the Lord Jesus selected these adjectives Himself, we need to look at them a little closer. The King James Version translated the word "gentle" as "meek,"[1] while the New American Standard Bible preferred the word "gentle." What a contrast from the Pharisees of Jesus' day who appeared to be proud, arrogant, and self-righteous. Yet Jesus Christ, the beloved Son of the heavenly Father, who existed with the Father in perfect union from eternity past, chose to describe Himself as gentle and humble. His choice helps me love Him all the more! How about you? Psalm 29:9 says, "And in His temple everything says, 'Glory!'" In other words, if you were able to travel all over heaven, you would notice every heavenly being everywhere proclaiming Christ's glory. Yet, He calls Himself gentle and humble in heart. How wonderful He is! Jesus is gentle, yet all powerful; meek, yet mighty in protecting His children; lowly, yet so glorious in His beauty that heavenly beings have to cover their faces in His presence. How privileged we are that He invites us to share His yoke with Him!

Do you know Christians who have walked in the yoke with the Lord—not perfectly but consistently—for five or six decades? Their kindness and loving spirit is attractive and it draws you like a magnet. You love being near them. Maybe they are a deacon in your church or your godly grandmother. The first part of 2 Corinthians 3:18 describes this phenomenon: "But we all, with unveiled face beholding as in a mirror the glory of the Lord." The apostle Paul has just been speaking, in verse thirteen, of how Moses' face glowed as a result of being in the very presence of God. He then addresses all born again Christians. It is as if we, who are experiencing God's rest, are staring into a mirror where we see the glory of Jesus Christ reflected in our faces. It is His kindness, His gentleness, His thoughtfulness, and His sweet spirit. It is nothing that we can personally take credit for, since it is *Christ's life reflected in us*. Can a full moon take credit for its light? Certainly not, because the moon is simply reflecting the light of another celestial body. If we believers in Jesus Christ will choose to enter Jesus' yoke, or in other words, enter God's rest, He promises to live His life through ours. This truth is life-changing once we realize that only Jesus can live His life through us. It's His power and His character.

In this same verse, Paul says, "[We] are being transformed into the same image from glory to glory." I love the verb *transformed*. While in the yoke with Christ, by faith, it is as if we watch in a mirror a process of spiritual metamorphosis taking place. Miracle of miracles, we observe ourselves being transformed *into the same image* as Christ.

Is this principle too much for you to take in? That is often the way it affects me, even though I have read it many times. Could it be true that in the yoke with Jesus Christ I become transformed into the very image of His life? Yes, that's exactly what Paul is saying and it is reflected glory, not our own. A well-known cult teaches that we can become literal gods, but that is not what the Bible is teaching here. Who facilitates this whole transformation process? The end of verse 18 says, "just as from the Lord, the Spirit." It is God the Holy Spirit who does it. We are responsible to walk quietly in the yoke with Jesus Christ and He through the Spirit does it all.

AND YOU SHALL FIND REST FOR YOUR SOULS

Do you have a personal Bible verse that you return to in stressful times? Del and I do. It did not come by running our fingers down a heartwarming chapter of Scripture and randomly picking one. Rather, the verse became the bedrock of our shared faith because of crises of fear, doubt, and disappointment.

Within the space of four or five months, Del and I went through some life crunching experiences that produced a great deal of stress in our young marriage. Del was twenty seven years old and I was twenty eight. I was a veterinarian working as Director of Quality Control for a small drug company in Wisconsin. Through a series of circumstances that only God could have orchestrated, Del and I met several couples who were training to be church planting missionaries with New Tribes Mission. NTM had several missionary training centers and one of them was only fifteen miles from our town. As we got to know these missionary candidates, the simplicity of their walk of faith and their openness about what God was teaching them struck a chord in our hearts.

We also attended an NTM missionary conference held annually at Camp Awana, north of Milwaukee. Stories of people taking the gospel of Jesus Christ to primitive tribal groups around the world, who had never once heard the name of Jesus, resonated with us.

In March of 1969, we applied to take the NTM missionary training course and were accepted. Shortly after, I resigned my job, much to the horror of both sets of parents, and we set our faces toward being missionaries.

I cannot thank the Lord enough for the loving, loyal wife He gave me. Del was twenty-three when she trusted Jesus to be her personal Savior, so she knew very little about missions or missionary life. As for me, our family had hosted missionaries in our home when I was a boy. From what Del could piece together, at least in the beginning, being a missionary meant going to Africa and automatically dying there. This was stressful for her, and the fact that she was expecting our second child about the time we were supposed to begin missionary training only added to her uncertainty. Del sorted our belongings—those to be sold in a rummage sale, those to go with us, and those to be given away. On August 21 she delivered our precious daughter Terry, much to our great joy and the delight of our two-year-old daughter Kelley.

A few days later, we netted $700. at our rummage sale. This money had to last, we thought, for the rest of our lives because we were joining a faith mission and would not be receiving a salary. In time we came to understand that our financial needs would be met by God standing behind the promises of His Word. This was a brand new concept for us. Looking back, I realize that this principle of trusting God to supply our needs was not only an essential part of missionary training but also of the Christian life in general. The apostle Paul wrote, "And my God shall supply *all* your needs according to His riches in glory in Christ Jesus [emphasis added|" (Philippians 4:19). For Del and me, the truth of this verse was about to go from theory to reality.

At this time, I was full of my own importance. In the months leading up to us entering the training I can still remember thinking—and I'm embarrassed to admit it—that it would not take the NTM staff long to realize what a prize they had in me. Most likely they would want me to be a mission representative rather than having me take the training like the rest of the missionary candidates. They would probably ask me to travel to local churches to speak about NTM while my wife took the missionary training.

Our little family of four set off, pulling a trailer with all of our worldly goods, headed to the missionary training center in Durham, a small town in rural Ontario, Canada. We were assigned an apartment of two small rooms for the twelve month training program—a kitchen-living room and one bedroom that soon became wall-to-wall beds. Baby Terry slept in a bassinet and two-year-old Kelley slept in a crib.

I was in my glory! We had stepped out by faith in obedience to Christ's great commission, "But you shall receive power when the Holy Spirit has come upon you; and you shall be My witnesses both in Jerusalem, and in all Judea and Samaria, and even to the remotest part of the earth" (Acts 1:8). We were depending on His promises that He would take care of us. Del was not yet over the postpartum blues, but in the two weeks since her delivery she had organized our packing, a rummage sale, and the set up of our new apartment. I was so self-absorbed that I didn't stop to think about the toll on her—of me quitting my job, the birth of our second child, the move, the money, and the totally new way of life.

I loved the whole training atmosphere. I had left the secular business world behind and I was relishing being with other missionary candidates who also wanted to serve the Lord. What could be better short of being in heaven? But in my self-centeredness, I was insensitive to my dear wife. She was struggling, and understandably so—I was missing all the signals. We would have classes all morning. After lunch, the men and single women were involved in maintenance projects on the school property which housed about forty-five students and four staff families. When work ended for the day, most of the men would gather to play touch football.

One evening, about two weeks into the training, I came home to our little apartment after playing football, fully expecting to find a Norman Rockwell picture of family bliss—Del with an apron on, the children playing and laughing on the floor, while supper cooked deliciously on the stove. That was not the picture that confronted me. Almost forty years later, I can still see my dear Del sitting in a rocking chair, holding four-week-old Terry, tears streaming down her face, with no sign of dinner in the immediate future. She greeted me with, "I don't want to be here! I don't belong here! I want to go home!"

My dream of missionary training must have drained out of my heart as the color drained out of my face. I stood there clueless! I didn't know much but I knew we were finished as far as being missionaries. Two weeks into the course and we were done! Now we would repack our boxes and have to face our parents who we knew would never say, "I told you so," but would probably be very relieved.

I sat down and cried next to Del having no idea what to do or say. We were both frustrated and discouraged. I went for a walk and remember telling the Lord that I was at the end of my resources; I didn't know how to help my wife—or myself for that matter. Our future looked like an abysmal failure. I returned to our little apartment with a phrase from a Bible verse flitting in and out of my mind. At first I wasn't sure where to find it, but with the help of a concordance I finally located it in Isaiah, chapter 41. I returned to Del, still sitting distraught in her rocker and I pulled a chair up beside her. Feeling so helpless and inadequate, I prayed with her, and then slowly read this verse—a verse that became our family shelter:

> "Do not fear, for I am with you;
> do not anxiously look about you, for I am your God.
> I will strengthen you, surely I will help you,
> surely I will uphold you with My righteous right hand"
> (Isaiah 41:10).

There was no clap of thunder but Del and I knew for certain that Jesus Christ had intervened to minister His lovingkindness to two of His very needy children. We were starting out on a serious walk of faith and this was a crucial decision time. If we had walked away at this point, I think we would have had trouble mustering the faith to step out like this later on. In some way, we had planted our family standard on the rock of God's Word.

We dried our tears, Del changed the baby, and got supper ready. We knew we had experienced a major spiritual victory. We had turned a corner and it had all centered on God's precious Word. The victory was His and the blessing was ours! We were beginning to learn about God's rest. There have been many more heavy situations in subsequent years, but when Del and I return to the familiar ground of Isaiah 41:10, we continually find the same comfort and strength from our heavenly Father that we did on that day.

FOR MY YOKE IS EASY, AND MY LOAD IS LIGHT

Jesus delights in providing His children with good things beyond their imaginations. He communicates to us in Matthew 11:29 that not only is the outcome of being yoked with Him wonderful, but the process in reaching that outcome is also a rich blessing. We recoil at the sight of a yoke and we think that our rights and our independence are going to be violated. If it is a yoke, it must mean bondage, labor, pain, and yes, someone else making all the decisions for us. So we wrongly conclude that there must be a better way that does not involve putting our necks through a confining yoke, even when our partner is the Son of God. The Lord Jesus seems to say to us, "Go ahead! Trust me! Have I ever offered something to you that you did not come to see was wonderful, as you grew and matured? I love you. I have too much invested in you to hurt you. You are precious to Me. Go ahead and slip the yoke over your neck. It looks heavy but it's actually light and pleasant." The enemy of our souls may offer us choices that appear to our human eyes to be pleasant but turn out to be destructive. Our heavenly Father, by contrast, offers us choices that at first may appear hard and confining but turn out to be positive and constructive.

    I would love to have been there when the young bull from the previous illustration was in the yoke with that mature ox. I would also love to have been able to talk straight to him so that he would have heard and understood me—something like, "You are beating yourself to death on that wooden yoke, aren't you? Can I tell you something simple that will make the whole process of pulling that cart so much easier? You have basically two choices. You can keep resisting that yoke by twisting and trying to sit down. But the cart and the yoke are going forward and they can either drag you along or you have one other excellent choice. Your partner there, the faithful ox on the other side of the yoke, is doing all the pulling. And right now she is even pulling you. You could simply *rest* in the yoke, and if you walked along at the same speed you would barely even feel the yoke. Your partner is prepared to do all the heavy pulling. I sure hope you will make the right choice. You will actually find it to be a comfortable—even pleasant—experience."

CHAPTER SIX – THEMES FOR FURTHER STUDY

- The Lord Jesus gives us the choice to yoke ourselves with Him or not. He doesn't make us do His will. (Matthew 11:29)

- Choosing to share Christ's yoke is about a *relationship* with Him and not a *place*. (Matthew 11:29-30)

- In one of the few verses in the New Testament where Jesus describes Himself, He chooses from all of His attributes to highlight that He is *gentle* and *humble in heart*. (Matthew 11:29)

- As we "log time" resting in Jesus Christ, it's not that we learn how to imitate Him—rather His life is *reflected through us*. It is a metamorphosis! The net result is that we are transformed into the same image as Christ. (2 Corinthians 3:18)

- This miraculous process is accomplished by the Holy Spirit working in us, as we rest in Christ. (2 Corinthians 3:18)

- The thought of sharing a yoke, even with God's Son, sounds like a loss of independence. It's actually just the opposite—it's liberating. Jesus promises us that His yoke is light, not heavy. (Matthew 11:30)

Chapter 7

THE GREATEST VINE IN THE WORLD

When the unique invitation arrived in the mail, my wife and I were both amazed and excited. We were invited to a relative's wedding in the middle of a vineyard. The ceremony took place outside on the patio of the main building that was surrounded by hundreds of acres of neatly arranged rows of grapevines. Afterward, we were taken on a tour and saw the whole winemaking process. We saw where the grapes were unloaded from the rows of vines; the stage of converting the sweet pulp to wine; and finally the aging room where the wine rested in oak casks for a prescribed period of time at a strictly controlled temperature. Watching these intricate procedures firsthand made Christ's miracle at the wedding at Cana even more marvelous to me. Jesus spoke and plain water became the very best wine—possibly the best ever tasted by the human race.

Similarly, when I think of God's rest, John 15 invariably comes to mind. Other conversations in the Gospels may give a sentence or two about this subject, but John chapter 15 is like the mother lode of truth concerning what it means to enter God's rest and what benefits are ours when we pursue it. So, grab your pick, your pan, and your shovel, and walk with me through the first part of this chapter, asking the Holy Spirit to open up the wonder of His glorious truth to our hearts so that we will be enriched spiritually beyond our wildest expectations.

Jesus had demonstrated His servant-heart by washing His disciples' feet before they shared the Lord's Supper together. Then He lovingly prepares His followers for the tumultuous events ahead with the words, "Let not your heart be troubled; believe in God, believe also in Me" (John 14:1). In verse 27, we read that Jesus comforts them by saying, "Peace I leave with you; My peace I give to you; not as the world gives, do I give to you. Let not your heart be troubled, nor let it be fearful."

Can you picture yourself there hearing the Son of God with all the glory of heaven confined in the body of a Nazarene carpenter, telling you that you can experience true peace—God's peace, because the Holy Spirit will be available to you continually? He tells you not to let your emotions take control of you and not to be afraid. There is nothing of so great a severity that your heart should be fearful. Why? Because He is the Prince of Peace who is prepared to fill your life with His strength and security.

As He so often did, Jesus used an illustration in chapter 15 that was culturally understandable for the disciples. They had watched their own parents making wine for their family's daily needs and understood well what grapes needed to be healthy and productive.

Do you know where the world's oldest and largest grapevine continues to grow? You will find the Great Vine in Hampton Court Palace Gardens in England. We are told that it was planted in 1768 and its girth in 1800 was about twelve inches. By 1887, the circumference around the base was four feet and it currently measures twelve feet. The longest runner is a whopping 120 feet. When the yearly crop is ready for picking in September, it takes the vinedresser three weeks to remove all the grapes. The crop averages 500 to 700 bunches of grapes. The largest harvest was 2,245 bunches in 1807.[1]

Jesus likens Himself in John's Gospel to the vine's main structure—the root, the base, and the trunk. We who are followers of Jesus Christ are portrayed as branches connected to Him. What part does His Father, the God of heaven, play? He is the gardener, the vinedresser, the husbandman, and the caretaker. He is also the one who owns the vineyard; the fruit belongs to Him and is for His benefit.

Verse two of chapter 15 is often misunderstood because of the expression, "He takes away." It has been erroneously taught that if a branch (a born-again child of God) sins or does not bear spiritual fruit, God takes us away or somehow cuts us off. Is this the God of the Bible that we have come to know; the God of Israel who worked patiently and painfully with the Jewish nation despite their repeated disobedience? Is that how we parents train up our children? The first time they mess up, do we cut them off from the rest of the family? How much less likely is the God of all love, who sent His Son to take our place on the Cross, inclined to cut us out of His spiritual family because of a sin? This beautiful truth draws my heart closer to my dear heavenly Father. He is the vinedresser who loves His plants (us). He is determined to nurture us into spiritual maturity.

Picture a typical Galilean man of Jesus' day who has a small patch of grapevines at the back of his humble dwelling. Every morning he walks between the rows once the grapes begin to appear on the vines—small, green, immature grapes. He has almost finished inspecting the last row when his eye catches a vine that is supposed to be hanging across the supporting twine. Instead, it's sprawled in the dirt! He recognizes hoof prints and realizes his neighbor's donkey has escaped again and run through his vineyard. A hoof print still presses a branch into the ground. The vinedresser immediately gets down on his knees, his face almost in the dirt, to assess the trauma. It is torn but not completely. Ever so carefully he lifts the branch, blows off the dirt so as not to bruise it further, and supports it with two hands as he lays it over the twine where it had once rested. From his robe he takes a little leather pouch that he always carries with him, containing a healing ointment. Gingerly, he layers the thick paste over the area where the bark has been peeled back. The ointment will keep the insects from taking advantage of this fresh wound to penetrate the branch and eventually kill it. The plant will get extra portions of fertilizer and water and be carefully scrutinized many times each day. As Jesus detailed this parable, each disciple in the room would have grasped the loving concern of the vinedresser.

Let's consider an interesting phrase in verse two that often causes misunderstanding. The Greek word *airo* that is translated "takes away" also means, "to raise or lift." This same word is also found in other verses in the Greek New Testament. The emphasis is added in each example:

- Luke 17:13–"And they *raised* their voices"
- John 11:41–"And Jesus *raised* His eyes, and said"
- Acts 4:24–"And when they heard this, they *lifted* their voices to God"
- Revelation 10:5–"And the angel whom I saw standing on the sea and on the land *lifted up* his right hand to heaven."

In John 15:2, it makes more sense in the context to translate *airo* as *bear up* or *lift up* than *take away*. Both are allowable meanings of this one Greek word, but in this context Jesus is teaching His disciples about the loving, caring heart of God the Father. He tends and cares for the branches when they are down in the dirt; He raises them and cleans them off; He supports them and protects them from further damage.

The Father makes sure they have extra mulch and water so that they can join the other branches on the joyous day of harvest. The Gospel of John speaks of this same Vinedresser, "For God so loved the world, that He gave His only begotten Son, that whoever believes in Him should not perish, but have eternal life" (John 3:16).

Do we honestly believe that the eternal Vinedresser walks around His vineyard with a machete rather than a container of salve? When He spots a branch not bearing fruit—*whack*! Off comes the branch! No! God the Father is more like the shepherd I read about in Luke 15:1-7. When one of His hundred sheep comes up missing, He doesn't say, "Good riddance! That sheep was a real problem to me anyway." Verse 4 of Luke 15 tells us that He leaves the ninety-nine and goes after the lost one, "until he finds it." That little phrase gives indescribable comfort to me. It tells me that I may fall into sin or in some way disobey God, but He will go looking for me—He will never quit pursuing me. Verse 5 assures us, "And when he has found it, he lays it on his shoulders, rejoicing." Notice it doesn't say, *if* he finds it but rather *when* he finds it. God will not stop hunting us down, lifting us up, applying the salve, forgiving our sin, and hugging us on His shoulders. Does this not speak deeply to your heart about how divinely possessive God is about His redeemed children?

Verse 6 is just as thrilling! "And when he comes home, he calls together his friends and his neighbors, saying to them, 'Rejoice with me, for I have found my sheep which was lost!'" Jesus then describes the joyous celebration that takes place in heaven because one—maybe it was you or me—had a change of mind and turned in thankfulness to the loving, searching chief Shepherd.

During a period of my life, I was that one. While in college, I rebelled against God, choosing to live like an unbeliever. I knew that I was saved, having trusted Christ as my Savior when I was seven years old. I made all kinds of excuses and blamed God that He had made me like I was. I wasn't experiencing the joyful, peace-filled life of a believer in fellowship with God, and because I sensed the restraining hand of God's Spirit, I could not enjoy the life of sin either. It was the worst of both worlds. I fully expected God to one day throw the maximum punishment at me—maybe I would suffer a broken neck in an auto accident. Then we would be *even*. That was my foolish understanding of God and how He works with His children.

The beautiful part of my own story is that He left the ninety-nine and went looking for me. Some say that it was the custom of shepherds in Jesus' day to purposely break the straying sheep's leg and then carry the sheep around until the leg healed in order to teach it not to stray. I don't read that in Luke 15. The shepherd in that chapter looks for his wayward sheep until he finds it and then "He lays it on his shoulders, rejoicing."

Please don't miss this wonderful principle of our gracious heavenly Father. His loving heart will keep Him looking and pursuing until He finds us. That was exactly how God dealt with me. I was expecting Him to one day say, "That's enough!" and punish me severely. I was waiting for God's hammer of justice to fall—or maybe His machete. Instead, He overwhelmed me with His tender love and mercy. I wasn't prepared for that and His grace broke my heart.

When I graduated from college, I was a new veterinarian; single and on my way to my first job as an instructor at the Veterinary College at Michigan State University. I felt that I was really something! In reality, I was one of God's flock who was blind, self-willed, and wandering off on my own. Within a few months, I was dating a schoolteacher who didn't know Jesus. Our conversation eventually got around to what we believed about God. I could sense that she had a tenderness toward God the Father and His Son, but she did not know the way of salvation. I had been away from God and His Word for such a long time that I wasn't able to open a Bible to John 3:16 and explain it to her. I was coming to love Del deeply and I knew that she needed to become a Christian by faith in Christ's death. I had wandered from the Lord for a long time and lacked familiarity with the Bible. God brought a faithful pastor and his wife into my life. I introduced Del to the pastor's wife and they spent many Saturday afternoons together, Del asking questions and Lois answering them from God's Word.

At some point along the way, Del put her trust in Christ's sacrifice for her and became a Christian. Her new joy and freedom in the Lord drew me back to Christ. Jesus, the searching Shepherd, flooded my life with His grace. He had not given up! He put me on His shoulders. He said, "Rejoice with me, for I have found my sheep which was lost!" My eyes brim with tears of joy and thankfulness even now as I relive that situation.

Jesus uses several word pictures in John 15 that require our attention:

- THE VINE – Jesus Christ, God's Son

The vine is anchored into the ground, making it secure and keeping the rest of the plant from blowing away. The branches are elevated so they can get maximum light and moisture. The roots of the vine absorb only those chemicals, minerals, and fluids that will nourish the branches and prepare them to produce a bumper crop of grapes. The nutrient-filled sap flows up the length of the vine and enters each branch. It always moves toward the branches.

- THE BRANCHES – All born again believers in Jesus Christ

The branches are not responsible to select the ingredients that help form the grapes. That is the vine's responsibility. The key to producing fruit is the point of union or connection where the branch attaches to the vine. All the nutrients have to pass through that point of *relationship*. The branch is only as secure as the vine to which it is joined.

Some years ago, the strength of that point of connection between the vine and the branches became very real to me. I had just heard teaching on John 15 and the parable of the vineyard. I was sawing a board that had several knots in it and was becoming frustrated because my saw kept catching in the knots. Then it struck me—the knot is where the branch attaches to the vine or trunk. It is the hardest, densest wood on the tree because of the strength required for the trunk to hold onto the branch. If the connection is weak, the branch will break off from the trunk, its source of nutrition, strength, and protection. Branches are *displayers of fruit*—expressions of the work that the vine does. The branch increases in fruitfulness until it is time for the harvest.

- THE VINEDRESSER – God the Father

Not only does the vinedresser care for the injured plants, but he also prunes the branches that are loaded down with ripe fruit. In the same fold of his robe where he carries the container of salve for the *hurting* branch, he carries a cutting tool for the *fruitful* branch—not to permanently cut branches away from the vine, but to snip off nonproductive shoots that drain life and nourishment.

Vines are not the only plants that require pruning—many flowers do also. Anyone who has grown roses knows that in order to get big gorgeous blooms you have to cut back the rose bush, sometimes quite drastically, in order to concentrate the nourishment where it will be the most productive. My dad loved to grow roses and he was good at it. I can still hear him talking about sucker branches that would never grow flowers but only draw off essential nutrients.

What was Jesus describing when He talked about God the Father pruning His children? It helps enormously in understanding any passage of Scripture to be constantly aware of the *context* or setting of the verse. John 15 is not dealing with how to know Jesus as one's Savior. It's addressing branches (believers) who are part of the Vine (Jesus Christ) and also with *fruit bearing* that results from abiding or resting in Jesus—something that cannot pertain to unbelievers or unsaved.

In the second part of verse 2, we see another aspect of how God delights to work in His children's lives. If they are walking in obedience to Him and bearing spiritual fruit, He will not be content to leave them at that level of maturity. Our heavenly Father's goal is to see us grow in the likeness of His beloved Son. For that to happen, Jesus, who dwells inside each believer by the Holy Spirit, must live His life out through that child of God more and more. Therefore, our loving Father allows a mix of both pleasant and difficult experiences into our lives. This is the Father's pruning process! The apostle Paul expressed it this way, "I know how to get along with humble means, and I also know how to live in prosperity; in any and every circumstance I have learned the secret of being filled and going hungry, both of having abundance and suffering need" (Philippians 4:12). How does our heavenly Father want us to respond to Him in the prosperous times and the times of loneliness and failure? By depending on Him and His Father-love, because of what He says about Himself in Scripture. I have already shared how Isaiah 41:10 came to be our family verse. In times of adversity, when Del and I have held on to this verse by faith, we have grown spiritually rather than turn on each other with blame and anger and thus fail to bear spiritual fruit.

What is the fruit about which verse 2 speaks? I believe the Bible clarifies this in Galatians 5:22-23: "But the fruit of the Spirit is love, joy, peace, patience, kindness, goodness, faithfulness, gentleness, self-control; against such things there is no law." Not surprisingly, these qualities describe the personality of Jesus Christ. These nine attributes are like grapes that make up one cluster of delicious fruit.

In verse 4 of John 15 we come across this wonderful word *abide*, which I believe is a synonym for God's rest. It speaks of that place of intimacy between our heavenly Father and us, the children of His love. This relationship is one of mutual abiding—we in Him and He in us. Using the simple illustration of the vine, the branch, and the fruit, Jesus teaches us that we are not capable of living a life that consistently pleases God the Father by ourselves. Only Jesus can! We cannot bear spiritual fruit without abiding in the Son any more than a branch can grow grapes without being connected to the vine. Believers display the life of Jesus Christ when they are abiding in Him who is their source of spiritual vitality.

How does this principle of abiding affect you? These verses always set my heart at rest. For more years than I care to remember, I strove to live the Christian life—to do the right spiritual thing at the appropriate time and to be at peace in the midst of my own personal storms. Once I began to understand the truth of abiding in Jesus—resting in Him—I felt like someone was lifting a huge weight off my shoulders and I began to sense a freedom of spirit about which I had only read. God was holding out a promise to me, saying, "Why do you struggle? I am only looking for My beloved Son's life in you—not a human substitute. Just abide in Him by faith, and His life will flow out through you. Others will see the life of Jesus in you!"

The apostle Paul describes so well this phenomenon of Christ living His life through the abiding child of God. *The Amplified Bible* states, "For we are the sweet fragrance of Christ [which exhales] unto God, [discernible alike] among those who are being saved and among those who are perishing: to the latter it is an aroma [wafted] from death to death [a fatal odor, the smell of doom]; to the former it is an aroma from life to life [a vital fragrance, living and fresh]" (2 Corinthians 2:15-16a).[2]

Let's make the choice to abide in Christ. Let's allow Him to live His life in us. Then we will impart His fragrance to others and all the glory will belong to Him.

CHAPTER SEVEN – THEMES FOR FURTHER STUDY

- There is no trial of so great a magnitude that we should be fearful since Jesus is our Prince of Peace. (John 14:1-6)

- Jesus drew a wonderful word picture in John 15 of abiding (resting) in Him. He is the main stem or trunk; His blood-bought children are the branches that bear His fruit; and God the Father is the owner/husbandman. (John 15:1-5)

- When God's children sin, God, the husbandman, does not cut them out of the family. On the contrary, He lifts them up, reinforces them, and nurses them back to a place of productivity and blessing. (John 15:2)

- Luke 15 illustrates clearly that when God's children are rebellious and turn away from Him, He pursues us relentlessly in love, until we have a change of mind, confess our sin, and return to His fellowship.

All of heaven rejoices when that rebellious "lamb" is found and returns home. (Luke 15:1-7)

- One of the grapevine's most strategic locations is where it connects with the branch. All the elements for producing fruit must pass through this point of union. (John 15:5)

- God the husbandman both nurses the *hurting* branch as well as prunes the *productive* branch, so that both will produce even more fruit. (John 15:2)

- God's pruning of His children involves times of prosperity and pain, so that through these testings we would learn to depend more and more on Him. (Philippians 4:12)

- The fruit of the Spirit that is listed in the Biblical epistles undoubtedly describes the personality of Jesus Christ. (Galatians 5:22-23)

- The word "abide" that Jesus uses in John 15 to describe the illustration of the vine, is synonymous with the word "rest" that is used elsewhere in Scripture. (John 15:5-7)

- Only Jesus can fully live the Christian life in ways that please the Father. The only way that we can experience the same life is by abiding/resting in Jesus Christ (the Vine). (John 15:5)

Chapter 8

FRUIT GROWING—101

I find it very interesting how many liberal journalists and news commentators visualize born again Christians and how they interpret the things we say. Although many of their descriptions are inaccurate, some of them, unfortunately, are true at times and when those are trumpeted in the media, we Christians wince. How very different these descriptions are from the way Jesus Christ describes the abiding life or God's rest.

Chapter 15 of John's Gospel lists at least eight glorious benefits that take place in the life of a Christian who chooses to abide in Jesus Christ. Verse 5 begins by explaining who the various participants are in this profound but simple illustration of the vineyard. Jesus tells us that He is represented by the *vine* which is made up of the root, the base, and the stem. He is the one through whom all the essential nutrients must travel if fruit is going to develop on the branches. There is no other way!

Next, the Lord tells us that every child of God is a *branch* that is connected to Him, the Vine. And then He makes a startling statement. Some of those branches remain connected to the Vine while other branches at times become disconnected—in other words, they cease to abide in the

Vine. Jesus is not addressing the subject of personal salvation but whether His saved children are bearing His precious fruit. To suggest that Jesus is talking about people gaining or losing salvation only complicates a wonderfully uncomplicated truth. After clarifying once again who the participants are in this illustration, Jesus summarizes the bottom line of this life-changing truth:

- *Abiding*, in Christ's mind, is a mutual relationship. He says, "He who abides in Me, and I in him" (John 15:5). How thrilling is that!
- The result of this abiding relationship is not that we bear *some* fruit but that we bear *much* fruit.
- If spiritual fruit is that which Christ accomplishes in us, then it stands to reason that Christians cannot produce it without a connection to the source, Jesus Christ.

A misunderstanding of John 15:6 has also resulted in confusion. It seems to be saying at first reading that if *anyone* (and the context here is believers), fails at any point in their life to abide in Christ, they are thrown away as a branch and dry up. Then, someone gathers up these ones who were thrown away and casts them into the fire and they are burned. We have to be very careful in our interpretation of this verse because if that is the correct meaning, then the first time we blow up in anger or have a lustful thought (both of which Jesus calls sins), we are headed for hellfire. Surely that cannot be what this verse means! If it were, it would contradict how the rest of Scripture pictures the way our loving heavenly Father tirelessly works in our lives to conform us to the image of His Son. Besides that, since Christians are not perfect, we all are prone to sin at some time or other. James writes, "For we all stumble in many ways" (James 3:2). Where confusion exists in Scripture, I believe we need to look to other Bible passages since Scripture is its own best interpreter. Two other passages should help us here.

The first is 2 Timothy 2:20-22. Once again the Holy Spirit uses an illustration for us to understand a vital Christian principle. Verse 20 speaks of "a large house" which helps us to realize that the context here is *believers*. The apostle Paul teaches that in the master's house, (God's family), there are vessels of gold and silver as well as vessels of wood and earthenware. The former group is called vessels *to honor* and the latter is vessels *to dishonor*. What makes this difference and why are there two groups? Does the master of the house have favorites—the gold and silver vessels? Is there also a group of lesser value that are not of the same quality—the wooden and earthenware vessels? Are there two kinds of Christians? Of course not! Then what makes the difference?

The explanation is clearly given in verse 21, where we read that the *vessels unto honor* are those who regularly cleanse themselves from "these things"—the wickedness (sin) referred to in verse 19. In other words, when a believer sins, the Holy Spirit convicts him of it. If he confesses that sin to God, our heavenly Father cleanses him of that sin. Verse 21 goes on to say that this genuine confession of sin results in the believer being sanctified (or set apart), useful to the master and ready for every good work. For a believer to keep from repeatedly sinning and ultimately becoming a "vessel unto dishonor" through whom the Lord would *not* be pleased to work, the erring one should be quick to confess and turn away from sin in his life. It doesn't make the forgiven believer a better or more beloved Christian but it does mean that God is pleased to use him to accomplish His will. This principle is fortified by verse 22 which instructs all believers to "Flee from youthful lusts, and pursue righteousness." Why? It assures a believer that God will delight to use him for His purposes.

I Corinthians 3:11-15 also brings out important truths that help us to better understand John 15:6. Verse 11 states, "For no man can lay a foundation other than the one which is laid, which is Jesus Christ." We know that our Christian life is built on Christ's death on the cross of Calvary, where He took our place and paid our debt of sin. All believers start the Christian life on an identical basis—eternal life based solely on Christ's work. But as Christians we make a host of choices every day of our lives. Verse 12 describes our various Christian activities as gold, silver, precious stones, wood, hay, and straw—basically two groups again. Activities that are done out of a wrong motive—pride, personal glory, or greed—are called wood, hay and stubble. Visualize a house made with wood and completely insulated with dry straw. Such a house pictures the life of a Christian who, because of a failure to abide in Christ and to consistently confess sin, has a life structure that is flammable to say the least. Of course they are still saved, but their *works* will not withstand the fiery judgment seat of Christ.

A life of Christian works resulting from the believer abiding in Christ is compared to gold, silver, and precious stones. This time picture a house built upon the foundation of Christ and constructed from these precious metals and gems. Such works will survive the fiery judgment of our Savior because they are His works, accomplished through the believer as a result of resting in Him. The "vessel for honor" will receive rewards for works that survive His judgment. What is gathered up in John 15:6 are the believer's *works* done in the power of human effort. Works that the Lord accomplishes through us while we are abiding in the Vine will last for eternity.

Earlier, I mentioned eight benefits in John 15 that God promises to the believer who consistently chooses to abide in Him. Talk about a benefits package that is out of this world!

- ANSWERED PRAYER (verse 7) – Jesus states that if believers will choose by faith to abide in Him, they can make requests through prayer to God and He will honor them. As we continue choosing to abide, our hearts begin to desire His pleasure rather than our own. James 4:3 states this contrast well: "You ask and do not receive, because you ask with wrong motives, so that you may spend it on your pleasures." Jesus Christ promises in His Word to answer my prayers when I choose to abide in Him and so I accept that thankfully. How He specifically answers I am content to leave with Him.
- GOD THE FATHER IS GLORIFIED (verse 8) – It may be hard for us to understand what is meant by God receiving glory because it doesn't seem to relate to us personally. We might even think that this is a transaction that takes place in heaven. We are glad it is happening but we're just not sure what is involved. Isn't God infinitely glorious already? How could something that we finite creatures do result in our omnipotent heavenly Father receiving more of anything? I don't pretend to know the answer, but the Bible speaks quite a bit about Jesus Christ and the Father being glorified.

In the Old Testament, we catch glimpses of God's shekinah glory descending upon and leaving various Hebrew structures of worship—a visible indication of His pleasure or displeasure with Israel's behavior. Jesus explains in verse 8 that if we will choose to abide in Him by faith and thus bear spiritual fruit, our heavenly Father will receive glory. I think that rather than us adding to God's glory, since He is perfect and infinite in all of His attributes, we can draw attention to the glory He already has. God the Father, the Son, and the Holy Spirit are the only ones to whom we can use the words *worthy of glory*. In Revelation 4 we read about the apostle John being physically translated into the throne room of Almighty God and visualizing all the glories of heaven. He then returns to earth and explains in human words what he saw. The Holy Spirit, through John, describes God's voice (verse 1), God's throne (verse 2), God Himself (verse 3), those sitting around God's throne (verse 4), the Holy Spirit (verse 5), heavenly beings who serve God (verses 7-9), and the twenty-four elders (verse 10)—possibly those who trusted Christ for salvation on earth.

- WE BEAR MUCH FRUIT (verse 8) – It is worth mentioning again the word *much* since it is used in verses 5 and 8. The Lord Jesus appears to be quantifying fruit bearing—by abiding in Him we will bear a bountiful harvest of spiritual fruit. I believe that the fruit John 15 refers to is *anything* that Jesus Christ accomplishes through the believer who abides in Him.

Sometimes the Lord allows us to see or hear where we helped another person. While abiding in Christ we may have said something that ministered to a fellow believer's unspoken need. It was exactly what their wounded heart needed and God's Spirit applied the specific balm of healing to that soul. Other times we may not hear how we were used by God—in the eternal scheme of things it's not really important. That's part of the deep blessing of abiding in Christ. There is no place for struggling to be a blessing to other people. We abide restfully as branches in our connection to the Vine, Jesus Christ, and we allow God to do His pleasure.

Let your eye run down the list of qualities again in Galatians 5:22-23. Wouldn't you agree that you know unbelievers who exhibit some of these qualities? Human effort is powerful and I have no doubt that certain personality types find it easier than others to be thoughtful, generous, joyful, or patient. When Jesus Christ talks about us bearing His attributes and virtues, which can only be received through abiding in Him, this is fruit of a different kind. This is eternal fruit! This is *much* fruit!

- WE PROVE THAT WE ARE JESUS' DISCIPLES (verse 8) – Who among Christian believers would not want to hear from God Himself that they are His *disciple*? Another benefit of abiding in the Lord Jesus is the proof that we are His disciples because of the spiritual fruit He enables us to bear. What does the word disciple mean? It's easy to remember Christ's twelve followers as disciples, but we are reluctant to think of ourselves with that title. However, Jesus has no difficulty in using that term. Jesus will work with us to see that we have every opportunity to grow in spiritual maturity and into His likeness.
- WE EXPERIENCE A DEEP AND INTIMATE LOVE RELATIONSHIP WITH JESUS (verses 9-10) – This is the benefit on which I most enjoy meditating. May your heart also be so filled with thankfulness for His Father-love that you will long even more for the depth of His communion. *The Amplified Bible* states, "I have loved you, [just] as the Father has loved Me; abide in My love [continue in His love with Me]" (John 15:9).[1] You and I cannot understand what the love of our heavenly Father is like for His beloved Son Jesus. We get hints of it when we read about Christ's baptism by John the Baptist. The Father in heaven spoke audibly, voicing His loving approval: "This is My beloved Son, in whom I am well-pleased" (Matthew 3:17). Yet Jesus unselfishly states that He loves us to the same extent that He loves the Father and the Father loves Him. This is awesome! I don't

think Jesus is saying that if a Christian abides consistently in Him that He will love him more than He loves Christians who struggle and fail. However, I do believe that Christians who spend the majority of their daily life abiding in Christ will enjoy a deeper level of intimacy with Jesus. They will also learn nuances of Christ's character that only He can reveal to hearts that are on the same spiritual frequency.

I love the way verse 9 ends in *The Amplified Bible*, "Continue in His love with Me."[1] This is nothing short of an *invitation* from Jesus Himself. Unselfishly, He invites us to revel in the heavenly Father's love as He pours it out upon His Son. Jesus urges us to come and experience the perfect love that He has enjoyed with His Father since eternity past. Toward the end of John 17, we find Christ praying thoughts that almost transcend human words: "Father, I desire that they also, whom Thou hast given Me, be with Me where I am, in order that they may behold My glory, which Thou hast given Me; for Thou didst love Me before the foundation of the world" (John 17:24). Perfect love existed between Father and Son long before earth with all its creatures and the universe itself were ever created. Since God is eternal, the Father's love never had a starting point. It is to this love that Jesus invites His children, while at the same time explaining that to fully enjoy that love we must abide in Him.

- FULLNESS OF JOY (verse 11) – I don't know anyone who would rather be miserable than full of true joy. On top of all the other benefits that abiding in Christ brings to the life of the child of God, our Savior tells us that He will do two things related to joy. The first is that He will put *His* joy inside us — not the world's happiness, but His divine joy. The second is that He wants our joy to be full to the top of our being—more than we can humanly imagine.

I shared earlier about my college years in Canada. As a Christian believer, I was determined to run my own life and make my own decisions rather than abide in Christ. I still graphically remember my lack of deep joy. Busy days of studying were punctuated with what I now recognize as foolishness—lots of superficial laughter and almost no joy. In my fourth year of the five-year course, I chose to be a Resident Assistant in a dormitory of younger students. I was twenty-two years of age, due to graduate as a veterinarian in another year, and I was totally miserable. I looked for my Bible one particular day and found it in the bottom drawer of my dresser. Alone in my room, I opened the Bible my parents had given me many years before. Not knowing where to read, I recall flipping from page to page. I don't know if I was expecting a voice from heaven to tell me where to look, or for my Bible to divinely fall open at some significant page. I was like a stranger wandering around in an unfamiliar neighborhood. What happened next took me completely by surprise.

I sat down on my bed and began to weep—not tears of repentance, but of frustration. I knew I was a child of God and yet I was miserable in my sinful lifestyle. I would like to say that this experience resulted in my getting down beside my bed, confessing my sin, and returning to the joy of fellowship with Jesus Christ. Unfortunately, that is not what happened. I stubbornly went on living in my own strength and wisdom.

- JESUS CALLS US HIS FRIENDS (verse 14) – It is important to emphasize that *all* born again Christians, whether they are thriving spiritually or are immature spiritually because of wrong choices, have the same *standing* before God. We are *all* redeemed sinners by His grace alone and we are *all* seated with Christ at the right hand of God the Father in heaven. Jesus makes a short but profound statement, "You are My friends, if you do what I command you." In the next verse the Lord Jesus explains in a little more detail what He meant. All who are born again are *servants* of our heavenly Father. The apostle Paul consistently referred to himself as a servant or slave of Jesus, as did Peter and James in their epistles. What a wonderful privilege to call ourselves servants of Almighty God. Surely that would be sufficient for us and as long as we lived, we would magnify God for being so generous. But Jesus teaches that when we as His branches abide in Him, the True Vine, we experience a relationship that staggers our imaginations. He sets aside the title *servant* and replaces it with the title *friend*.

The Amplified Bible brings out some delightful nuances of having a friend-to-friend relationship with Jesus Christ: "I do not call you servants (slaves) any longer, for the servant does not know what his master is doing (working out). But I have called you My friends, because I have made known to you everything that I have heard from My Father. [I have revealed to you everything that I have learned from Him]" (John 15:15).[2] Isn't that the most gracious promise that we could imagine? Jesus Christ is powerful enough to speak the entire universe into place and able to keep each atom functioning as it's supposed to. And yet He tells us that if we Christians will choose to abide in Him by faith that He will do something that a person only does with a *friend*—share everything with us. He promises to hold nothing back until there are no secrets between us. Can you think of one good reason why you wouldn't want to enjoy that kind of abiding relationship with Jesus Christ, the beloved Son of God?

- OUR FRUIT WILL REMAIN (Verse 16) – The eighth benefit of abiding in Christ should also be encouraging. Jesus promises that when He is allowed to bear His spiritual fruit through our lives, that it is eternal—it lasts forever: "You did not choose Me, but I chose you, and appointed you, that you should go and bear fruit, and that your fruit should remain" (John 15:16). This fruit is not like an ember in a fire that in time will cool and disintegrate, but it is everlasting along with our salvation and our heavenly home.

CHAPTER EIGHT – THEMES FOR FURTHER STUDY

- Scripture uses the words "gold, silver, and precious stones" to describe certain good activities that Christians accomplish (or, fruit that "branches" bear) as a result of resting in Christ. "Wood, hay, and straw" describe activities that are the product of *human energy*. When all of these works are one day tested by the Lord Jesus "with fire", only the former group will endure. (I Corinthians 3:11-15)

- At least eight benefits are mentioned in John 15 that come to believers who abide (rest) in the Vine (Christ):

    1. Our prayers are answered (v.7).
    2. God the Father is glorified (v.8).
    3. We bear *much* fruit (v.8).
    4. We prove that we are Jesus' disciples (v8).

5. We experience a deep and intimate love relationship with Jesus (vv.9-10).
6. Fullness of joy is ours (v.11).
7. Jesus calls us His *friends* (v.14).
8. Our fruit will remain (v.16)

Chapter 9

GOING OUT AND COMING IN—IT'S BY FAITH!

There is an axiom in life that is almost always true. If your phone rings at 1:30 a.m., it is serious and it is not *good* news. That was certainly the case in the wee hours of the morning on December 20, 1989. Once I became awake enough to realize that it was the phone, I got out of bed and made my way toward it in the dark. The first few words I heard were enough to snap my eyelids open, "This is Doug Hefft, the mission pilot calling! The U.S. military has invaded Panama! They have dropped bombs on the main Panama army garrison here in the capital and it's ablaze with fire! Also, I can hear gunfire all around our area of the city!"

I was still trying to shake the sleep out of my brain and my internal computer was not booting up very quickly. Fortunately, Doug was doing all the talking because I was really struggling to understand and put this startling new information together.

The United States invasion of Panama, code name *Operation Just Cause*, had begun and the U.S. military machine was about to respond to President Manuel Noriega's defiant ravings. The country of Panama had been slowly deteriorating in many ways and General Noriega was getting bolder and louder. Shortly before the U.S. invasion, Del and I had watched on television while Noriega challenged the U.S. even while he waved a machete in the air.

Rumors were everywhere of caches of guns from other countries being stashed around the Panama countryside. The president established what he called the *Dignity Battalion* which was primarily made up of criminals he released from prison. On trips into the capital, our family would often see in vacant lots groups of 150 or so of these men, still in their shabby street clothes, learning to march more or less in formation. This ragtag militia usually did their drills with broomsticks on their shoulders in place of guns. However, as the situation deteriorated, we heard that the Dignity Battalion members were issued AK-47s and given a free hand. We never knew when these vigilantes would suddenly put up a barricade to stop all traffic and take whatever they wanted.

University students reacted to the situation by burning cars and raising their own chaos. At serious times like this, there is often a sort of dark humor that in normal times would be hilarious. On a shopping trip to Panama City, we would often see black smoke rising from another batch of burning cars, so we would avoid driving in that area. Suddenly a convoy of Panama military vehicles would race by us, rushing to address this new demonstration. There would be trucks loaded with armed soldiers and usually one large black vehicle, something like a tank on regular truck tires. Painted on the side of this ominous black vehicle was a blue *Smurf*—a dwarfish character that was popular in the comics a few years ago. I have no idea what the connection was with the Smurfs but apparently this vehicle was a water cannon. According to the word on the street, the Panama military put dye in the water they sprayed on the rioting students to disperse them as well as to mark them for rounding up later.

Adding to the chaos, the banks froze all their accounts (including ours) by locking their doors. Economically, the Republic of Panama was quickly coming to a standstill, even while President Noriega was solidifying his power.

Prior to the invasion, we realized the U.S. military was doing some serious planning because large transport planes were flying over our house in the countryside around the clock. Two events seemed to light the fuse and give the U.S. strong reason for initiating the invasion. One was the picture on the TV screen of General Noriega challenging the U.S. to war. The other event appeared to strike the match. A group of U.S. soldiers from one of their military bases near Panama City had been eating at a restaurant in the capital. They were trying to drive back to their base after dinner but got lost in the heart of the city. As they approached one of the many barricades belonging to the Panama military, they panicked and decided to drive through the barricade rather than stop. As they raced through, a Panamanian soldier raised his weapon and shot through the back window of the American vehicle. A young officer was shot dead in the back seat. Although this was just an isolated incident, it seemed like the dominos had started to fall.

When *Operation Just Cause* began, U.S. paratroopers descended on the Panama City airport at the same time as the large Panama army garrison in the center of the city was being bombed. A smaller garrison on the edge of the old U.S. controlled Canal Zone that had a nativity scene on the front lawn, was reduced to a pile of cement blocks and twisted I-beams. The nativity scene was untouched even while the building next to it was leveled—an indication of the precision bombing. Once the invasion began, the Panama military fled and the capital city quickly descended into unbridled anarchy and lawlessness. This was the scenario behind our pilot calling us in the early morning, just hours after the invasion had begun.

The following days were very unsettling. Our mission had about seventy-five adults plus children in various parts of the country—some were living and working in remote tribal villages while others were in national towns. A two-hour drive west of the capital on the Pan-American Highway was the village of Chame, where our field office and missionary children's school were located. There were probably a hundred students, teachers, dorm parents, and support personnel living and working in the town. Rumors ran wild that the Panama military had dispersed throughout that small Central American country, and were settling old scores with Americans. A contingent of U.S. marines arrived discreetly by helicopter on the airstrip close to our house one night while hunting for a guerrilla group that was on the run.

We advised our missionaries to remain in their houses until we received some kind of an all clear from the U.S. Embassy. Our three children, who were all attending Liberty University in Virginia, had arrived in Panama for Christmas break two days before the invasion started. We were able to keep up with the news by watching CNN, so we left the TV on around-the-clock. The upside to all of this was that we had a lot of quality family time during our kids' Christmas vacation.

I would like to be able to report that our family's hearts were in a state of peaceful rest throughout this whole experience. That would *not* be the truth. We had never before been through the experience of staring down the barrel of a U.S. military invasion force and, furthermore, we had no idea how the invasion was going to end. We did turn to Isaiah 41:10 and prayerfully laid claim to its promises again and again. Our dear heavenly Father kept us safely through the invasion and its aftermath, as He did all of our foreign missionaries. Not a single injury was attributable to the war. Frankly, at times I had a lump of fear in my throat that I could not seem to swallow. Nevertheless, we kept on trusting our Savior; we kept on claiming Scripture's promises by faith; and we came out the other end with no visible scars.

I have a lot to learn about God's rest, but there is no question in my mind that such times of sheer panic serve to field test our Savior's wonderful promises of rest in the midst of crises. I am also coming to see that this relationship of abiding or resting, like the vine and the branches, is not a *thing* or an *experience* but rather a relationship with a *person*. It is all about Jesus Christ!

In discussing the topic of God's rest, it would be a major oversight to fail to look at Hebrews 3 and 4. It would be comparable to writing a comprehensive summary on the topic of baseball and never mentioning the World Series. The Holy Spirit, the author of Scripture, has given us a detailed picture in these two chapters of how God looks at His rest and the value He assigns to it in the lives of His children.

The context for these two delightful chapters is clearly stated in chapter 3, verse 1. By starting with the word, "Therefore," it means that the teaching that is coming is based on the previous teaching in chapters 1 and 2. The words, "Holy brethren, partakers of a heavenly calling," indicate that the author is speaking to true believers in Christ. Then the simple but profound phrase, "consider Jesus" urges us to stop and contemplate exactly what the Bible says about the Son of God. Doesn't it lift your spirit to realize that Jesus is "the Apostle and High Priest of our confession"? He is the one who came from heaven to earth to offer His blood as the only worthy offering to God the Father to pay for the sins of the world.

In verse 7, the author of Hebrews quotes five verses from Psalm 95:7-11. We have, as a backdrop to the teaching on God's rest, the Old Testament account of Israel leaving Egypt, wandering in the wilderness for forty years, and then entering into the Promised Land of Canaan. God could have used any story from the Bible or none at all, but He chose this detailed saga from Israel's history—of God's loving patience and Israel's stubborn willfulness.

In these five verses there are three major points, I believe, that God the Holy Spirit wants to drive home to our hearts. To emphasize these points, He repeats each of them several times.

- TODAY – There is no question that the Lord is communicating *urgency* to His children. The matter cannot wait until tomorrow morning. It is a *now* kind of truth. As soon as we become aware of it, He wants us to choose to put it into practice.
- DO NOT HARDEN YOUR HEARTS – Few believers would admit to having a hard heart even if we realized that we had not walked in obedience to God for many years. If, in the face of life's rigors, we refuse to rest in the Lord Jesus Christ by faith, then our hearts begin to get hard in self-sufficiency and stubborn pride. The longer we choose to resist abiding in the Vine, the more our spiritual hearts begin to set like concrete. Jesus wants to be everything we need all the time but He will not forcefully compete with us for control. He will graciously stand to the side and wait until we weary ourselves, all the while being perpetually available to us.
- I SWORE IN MY WRATH, THEY SHALL NOT ENTER MY REST – In order to underline how serious Jesus is about His rest, He tells us that His *righteous anger* is stirred up when His children refuse to enter by faith into the rest that He has freely provided for them. Say you are a mother who has worked very hard all afternoon to make your family's favorite meal. After giving thanks, everyone digs into the food on their plates—everyone, that is, but your eight-year-old son. He sits there with his hands in his

lap, staring at his food. "He must have the flu," you think to yourself, and so you ask him, "Are you not feeling well, son?" "Oh no," he answers, "I feel great. I'm just not sure of everything in this food. There may be something poisonous here that will harm me. I don't want to take the chance. I'll just do without this meal and tomorrow I'll examine the foods you serve closely to see if I think I can trust them." You say, "But honey, I'm your mom. I prepared this meal. I know everything that went into it and besides that, I love you, so you can at least trust my love." "Nope! Sorry, mom!" continues the son, "I know you mean well. But in the end, a person just has to depend on their own instincts."

Do you think that you might have just a twinge of hurt and anger in your heart? Likely, the anger would be less about the waste of good food and more about the unwillingness of your child to trust you, their loving, sacrificing parent.

Woven throughout Hebrews 3:7-11 and forming the framework for these three teaching points, is a stark description of *phase two* of Israel's trek from Egypt through the wilderness towards Canaan. The Holy Spirit sternly warns the Hebrew believers to whom He is writing, as well as to all believers generally, not to be like their forefathers. Their ancestors had tested God's graciousness, almost like a toddler tests his parents to see if there really is an endpoint to their grace. At what stage in his disobedience will his dad say, "That's it! No more grace! Now you are going to experience the pain of breaking the law!"

The Lord goes on to explain in verse 9, that Israel had no excuse for putting God to the test or for failing to trust Him. After all, the whole time that Israel was on their exodus, God was performing one miracle after another in order to demonstrate His loving care for them. Here are a few of those miracles:

- The Egyptian citizenry basically handed over their valuables to the Hebrews just before Israel started on their trip out of Egypt. (Exodus 12:35)
- God parted the Red Sea and destroyed Pharaoh and his entire army of charioteers. (Exodus 14:28)
- God wrote the Ten Commandments on stone tablets with His own hand. (Exodus 31:18)
- Fresh manna fell from heaven every morning for forty years. (Exodus 16:4)
- God provided quail by the ton when Israel grumbled about the manna. (Exodus 16:13)
- He poured water out of a rock in the desert, sufficient to satisfy several million Israelis and their livestock. (Exodus 17:6)
- God kept the clothing and shoes of the nation of Israel from wearing out for forty years. (Deuteronomy 29:5)
- He healed those who had been bitten by snakes and obediently looked toward a bronze serpent on a pole. (Numbers 21:8)
- God parted the Jordan River (in flood season no less) just before Israel was to enter Canaan. (Joshua 3:16)

The Holy Spirit writes that despite God miraculously meeting Israel's needs for forty years, they still tested the limits of God's grace by hardening their hearts and refusing to enter into His rest by faith.

The Lord voices a very strong condemnation of "your fathers," in verse 9. Being infinitely holy, God is not one to exaggerate either numbers of people or His response to their disobedience. Therefore, when He says, "They *always* go astray in their heart; and they did not know My ways (emphasis added)," He meant exactly that. It certainly was not because God failed to instruct Israel adequately during their forty years of wandering that they were always going astray. He was infinitely patient with them. Part of the reason for Israel's stubborn rebellion was that they did not know God's ways. They were willfully unfamiliar with the kinds of things that pleased Him, why they needed to depend on God every moment of every day, and why their worship of anything other than the Lord of Hosts Himself was such an affront to His character. In Hebrews 3 verse 11, He swore a divine oath or promise that any believer who refused to put their trust in Him and rest in who He is could not experience His divine place of rest.

Following the quotation from Psalm 95, the Lord immediately gives a somber warning to all Christians in the twelfth verse. He says, "Take care, brethren," confirming He is talking to His own redeemed children. Do you grasp the gravity of this warning—God, who knows everything, is telling us that we need to "take care"? Because God does not constantly warn us throughout the Bible, "Look out! Stop right there! Watch it! Be careful!" (even though we need Him to), it behooves us to pause and not proceed until we have specifically identified the danger He's alerting us to in verse 12. Only then should we proceed cautiously.

Well, we have stopped and we are now looking carefully around verse 12 to identify the serious danger that God knows is there. To what is God referring? We read, "Lest there should be in any one of you an evil, unbelieving heart, in falling away from the living God." We already saw that God is talking to "brethren," His own children. It is *family time* and our heavenly Father is giving us some strong instruction and warning. Please don't complicate the teaching here by thinking that "falling away from the living God" is talking about falling out of God's family because of our sin. We already clarified that in John 15. He uses the model of family to explain our relationship to Him. In our own families, do we disown our children when they disobey us? No, we discipline and teach them so they will mature and not keep failing in their areas of weakness. How much more unlikely, then, that our heavenly Father would ever disown us, considering that our eternal *birthright* was paid for with the precious blood of His own Son. We are eternally saved by God's grace through faith—as Christians, we also enter into God's rest by His grace through faith. The apostle Paul wrote, "As you therefore have received Christ Jesus the Lord, so walk in Him" (Colossians 2:6).

Instead of believers "falling away" or stubbornly trusting their own resources and failing to rest, the writer of Hebrews points out an amazing provision from God in chapter 3 verse 13. Nobody knows us better than our Creator and He seems to be saying here, "I know My children better than anyone does, and I know their default position is always to fall back on their own wisdom and strength—just like Israel constantly did in the wilderness. Therefore, besides the provision of My Holy Spirit who constantly convicts My children when they stumble, and My Scripture which clearly gives them instruction, I have designed a further means to keep them from missing out on My rest. Yes! It's the other members of My family."

"Really?" you say. "And how exactly is that supposed to help me enter into God's rest, rather than trust in my own discernment and experience?" Jesus Christ has designed His spiritual body to be formed from all born again believers with Him as the head. There is a wonderful picture of this harmony in the book of Ephesians where we read, "As a result, we are no longer to be children, tossed here and there by waves, and carried about by every wind of doctrine, by the trickery of men, by craftiness in deceitful scheming" (Ephesians 4:14). Isn't this how it was for us, before we came to know Jesus as our savior? We did not have the Holy

Spirit living inside us to give us His discernment. In many ways, we were subject to the unscrupulous dealings of an ungodly world system. However, once we were born again, we became members of His spiritual body with Christ as the head, guiding each function of His body according to the Father's will.

Many Christians have ignored Hebrews 3:13 and have built a case solely around Matthew 7:1 which reads, "Do not judge lest you be judged" as the reason why they cannot go and talk to a brother or sister in Christ who is enveloped in a sinful lifestyle. I have heard Christians say something like, "I know that brother is having an adulterous affair; or, this other Christian is an angry man who is gradually destroying his wife and children; or, this woman loves to gossip and is contributing to division within our church, but the Bible says that I am not supposed to judge other Christians, so I am not really free to say anything to them."

Do you honestly think that if the Holy Spirit showed us a fellow Christian caught up by the deception of sin who was consistently leading a life contrary to Scripture, that He would be upset if we followed Hebrews 3:13? We can pray and ask the Holy Spirit to give us the right words and attitude, and then kindly share with our brother or sister in Christ the truth concerning where they have erred. Jesus Christ outlined a very workable procedure to follow in the book of Matthew where He said, "And if your brother sins, go and reprove him in private; if he listens to you, you have won your brother. But if he does not listen to you, take one or two more with you, so that by the mouth of two or three witnesses every fact may be confirmed. And if he refuses to listen to them, tell it to the church" (Matthew 18: 15-17). God the Holy Spirit is going to be there convicting the one living in sin. However, if the sinning Christian continues to harden his heart and will not confess his sin to God, then it is the responsibility of the local church, as a united body, to ask that unrepentant brother or sister to leave the local fellowship until they do repent. Is it possible that we put too little value on the Spirit controlled fellowship and protection of the local church? Could it be that we grieve the heart of the Lord Jesus because we allow overt sin in our congregations to go unchecked?

Verse 13 of Hebrews 3 finishes by reminding us, "But encourage one another day after day, as long as it is still called 'Today,' lest any one of you be hardened by the deceitfulness of sin." I don't know how much importance the Lord wants us to put on the number of times a particular word is used in a Bible verse, but *today* is used five times in chapters 3 and 4 and *harden* four times. Nevertheless, the Lord plainly gives two reasons why He wants us to speak the truth to each other:

- *Sin is deceitful* – We may think we are wise and experienced enough to always recognize sin and avoid it. However, sin is deceitful and so are our own natural hearts. The prophet Jeremiah said, "The heart is deceitful above all things, and it is exceedingly perverse and corrupt and severely, mortally sick! Who can know it [perceive, understand, be acquainted with his own heart and mind]? (*The Amplified Bible*)" (Jeremiah 17:9).[1] Also, Satan is deceitful and he has been at this infernal temptation business for millenniums. He knows how to package sin so our easily deceived hearts jump at it.
- We must also speak the truth to each other in love because *sin hardens the heart*. I can recall that as a Christian teenager my heart was somewhat sensitive to the Holy Spirit's conviction when I did what I knew to be wrong. Even when I went off to college, as a freshman, my heart was still relatively conscious of God prompting me not to do certain things.

Unfortunately, I wanted my own way, so in time the sharp prick of conviction became the dull point of aggravation. Quite honestly, it became less uncomfortable to sin. Even as I recall these thoughts, I am ashamed to think that I would turn off the voice of the very Lord who bought me and paid for my sin with His blood. This, I believe, is what happens when our hearts become hardened, and is the very reason our dear heavenly Father warns us, "Take care!"

There is one more very important truth worth noticing in this story of Israel's painful forty-year trip from Egypt to Canaan and it is found in Hebrews 3 and 4. It is no accident that the trip falls into three segments, and each segment symbolically represents a different aspect of the Christian's life experience.

Egypt is commonly understood in Scripture to represent the unregenerate or unsaved condition. That is where the nation of Israel's journey began—in bondage and servitude, just like all mankind. We were all born as lost sinners under a death sentence. Salvation, then, is pictured by Israel coming out of Egypt and the enemy being defeated at the Red Sea. There is no going back to Egypt!

The second segment of the trip takes place in the *wilderness,* which is a picture of the believer living in the wasteland of the flesh or human effort. It is not where God intends the believer to live, since it is nothing but barrenness and frustration.

Finally there is Canaan—the land flowing with milk and honey. This is where God delights to have the believer live their Christian life. Canaan is not heaven, since Israel still had trials there; waged wars to displace the pagan residents; and often worshiped pagan idols. Deuteronomy 6 gives a detailed description of God's instructions to Israel right before their entrance into this fertile land. We read, "Then you shall say to your son, 'We were slaves to Pharaoh in Egypt; and the Lord brought us from Egypt with a mighty hand. Moreover, the Lord showed great and distressing signs and wonders before our eyes against Egypt, Pharaoh and all his household; and He brought us out from there in order to bring us in, to give us the land which He had sworn to our fathers'" (Deuteronomy 6:21-23). Canaan represents God's rest where by faith we are abiding in Him, just like branches abiding in the Vine. Did you notice as you read through Hebrews 3 and 4 how consistent Scripture is? The phrase "came out" (of Egypt), is only mentioned *once* (Hebrews 3:16), whereas the phrase "enter in" (to Canaan), is mentioned *eleven times*. We only need to be saved *once* but unfortunately, we tend to go back and forth between the wilderness and Canaan on a daily basis.

CHAPTER NINE – THEMES FOR FURTHER STUDY

- Abiding or resting in Jesus Christ is not a *thing* or an *experience* but a relationship with a person—Jesus Christ. In reality, the triune Godhead is involved. (Ephesians 3:20-21)

- God urgently desires that we enter His rest right now. That is why He repeats the word *today* five times in Hebrews chapters 3 and 4. (Hebrews 3:7,13, 15 and twice in 4:7)

- The Lord warns us four times in these same chapters that if we put off resting in Him, our spiritual hearts can become hard because of pride. (Hebrews 3:8,13,15 and 4:7)

- When we refuse to enter God's rest, it is an affront to His character and it stirs up His righteous anger. (Hebrews 3:10,17 and 4:3)

- God not only encourages believers through His Word and the Holy Spirit to embrace His rest; He also uses other members of the body of Christ. (Hebrews 3:13)

- God repeatedly warns us that *sin is deceitful*! Our hearts are easily tricked and Satan is a master deceiver. (Hebrews 3:13)

- Israel's history of their escape from Egypt into the wilderness, and eventually to the promised land of Canaan is a symbolic picture of the Christian life. *Egypt* is a picture of life before knowing Jesus as Savior; the *wilderness* is symbolic of the believer not abiding in Christ but walking in the flesh; and *Canaan* is a picture of the Christian living by the Holy Spirit's power in God's rest.

Chapter 10

DON'T HARDEN YOUR SPIRITUAL ARTERIES!

"Three of our missionary men, Dave, Rick and Mark, have been kidnapped by guerrillas!" I could not believe what I was hearing. Our mission pilot, Doug Hefft, stood in front of my wife and me with a white face and greasy coveralls, as we waited in the Panama immigration building for our visas. Every three months, all seventy-five missionaries working with New Tribes Mission in the Republic of Panama had to wait in a series of lines to get an immigration card with their picture on it, assuring another extension of their residence in the country. We had almost completed the three-hour process and were waiting for our cards when we saw Doug pushing his way through the crowd toward us. He stood out in the crush of people for several reasons. He was the only one we could see with a look of terror on his face, and his mechanic's coveralls clashed with the smartly dressed Panamanians. I was the NTM field director, so he felt that he should inform me as soon as possible. Doug wasted no time in telling his story and the jumble of details seemed to make no sense to us at all. Besides, it was Monday, February 1, 1993, and kidnappings of Americans just did not happen in

Panama—not at this time and especially not to missionaries. Finally, the links of the story began to form together into a chain of horrific events.

The previous day was a Sunday and in the early evening, a large group of guerrillas, proven later to be F.A.R.C. (*Fuerzas Armadas Revolucionarias de Colombia*) walked across the Panama border from Colombia and made their way through twenty miles of Darien jungle to the Kuna village of Pucuro. The three New Tribes Mission families who lived in Pucuro were involved in various aspects of missionary work in this Indian village of about 300 adults and children. It was dusk and the three families were resting in their hammocks at their respective jungle homes, when a portion of the guerrilla troop stormed into each couple's house armed with automatic weapons and tied up the three missionary men. Dave and Nancy Mankins and Rick and Patti Tenenoff had worked together for several years—Mark and Tania Rich, the youngest couple, were the newest members of the team. When each of the three men had their hands securely tied behind their backs, a guerrilla stepped outside each house and fired one shot—a signal to the others that their missionary man was subdued and tied up. The guerrillas and their three American captives crossed the Pucuro River next to the village, and disappeared into the blackness of the jungle. The rain forest absorbed them, and a surreal stillness was all that remained, consummating a carefully planned kidnapping that had been precisely executed in less than one hour. What would become of the three missionary men? What should the wives and their children do now? Should they flee or wait to see if their husbands would return? After all, the guerrillas had insisted that the wives should only pack enough clothing for their husbands for three days. How would the Kuna Indians of Pucuro react? Would they help the wives or through fear of the guerrillas turn against them?

In previous chapters, we read about God's rest as our dear Lord Jesus has described it in His own Word. My purpose in introducing this story of the multiple kidnappings of the NTM missionary men is to present an actual account of how three missionary wives experienced God's rest in one of the most nightmarish scenarios that any woman could imagine. These are not female *Christian action heroes*, but rather three normal Christian wives and mothers who, in a few seconds of time, were thrown into a crisis of monumental proportions, not knowing whether they would ever embrace their husbands again on earth. They had watched their husbands being thrown to the floor and tied up by armed men while others walked through their humble jungle dwellings taking whatever suited them. It wasn't long before these missionary wives realized that they had two choices, spiritually speaking:

1. They could resent the day they ever left the shores of the U.S.A. to help the indigenous people of a less fortunate country and could harbor bitterness against the God who took them there. They had given up so much and this was the reward they received—their husbands were brutally taken from them at gunpoint!
2. They could accept by faith rather than by feelings that they had given their lives to a *person* and not to a *job*. Their feelings could scream, "This isn't fair!" even while the Lord Jesus within them lovingly assured them, "Come to Me, all who are weary and heavy-laden, and I will give you rest" (Matthew 11:28).

Look again at the third chapter of the book of Hebrews. Verse 14 makes a staggering statement for anyone with an interest in growing spiritually and coming to know Christ more deeply. The first half of the verse states that we

Christians "have become *partakers of Christ* (emphasis added)." Can you think of any other religion whose adherents can become partakers of their deity? As far as I know, only Christianity makes this indescribable promise.

Remember that when we look at Bible verses that could possibly cause confusion, we need to look at the context or setting of the passage. We should carefully read several verses before and after the verse in question, paying special attention *to whom* the verse is being specifically addressed. In this case, the word "brethren" in verse 12 alerts us that only Christians are in view here. The context tells us that the author of the book of Hebrews is writing to encourage these scattered Jewish Christians to remember that in the midst of their persecution there is joy and peace only by entering into God's rest by faith. Any other choice is disobedience and unbelief—Israel's unfortunate preference en route from Egypt to the Promised Land.

Verse 14, therefore, tells us since Christians have God the Son living in them through the Holy Spirit, that entering into God's rest is not a business transaction but it involves partaking of the very life and nature of Jesus Himself. Is this resting in God an automatic experience for every Christian without any lapses from the moment of salvation straight through to death? The answer is clear—it's not automatic. That is one reason why the Lord gave us the book of Hebrews. The choice rests with us. Our Savior offers His rest as a *gift*, just as with salvation—but He doesn't *make* us accept either one. He even tells us what it will be like if we do *not* accept it—the account of the nation of Israel in the miserable wilderness. Fortunately for us, He also tells us graphically in John 15 what we can expect if we *do* enter by faith into God's rest. Every moment of every day of our Christian lives, we have the choice to either partake of Christ's life through entering into God's rest or to pull back and refuse God's divine offer.

What if I said, "My life is so crazy right now, I can't take the time to study this out for myself. I just don't have room for another thing in my hectic life"? Is the Lord likely to say, "Yes, I know all about your life. I can tell you that when your children are all in school, your life is going to even out some. You will be able to think more about My rest then. So until then, somehow survive!" That doesn't sound like the Lord, even though it could be the way you and I reason things out within ourselves. What Jesus does say about this matter of God's rest can be summed up in His poignant words in verse 15, "Today [for the 3rd time] if you hear His [God's] voice, do not harden [for the 3rd time] your hearts *(emphasis added)*." Wow! There just doesn't seem to be any wiggle room there for exceptions or excuses. It sounds like God is deadly serious. Just in case we need a real life illustration of what the Lord means, He details the picture again of the disobedient nation of Israel trekking through the wilderness.

I love the way that God dealt with men and women in the various stories in the Bible. He usually did not level a divine accusation at them when they sinned, even though being omniscient He could have done exactly that and been one hundred percent right in every detail. Instead, He often asked a penetrating question that appeared to bury itself deeply into the conscience and spirit of the individual. From His very first question to Adam in Genesis 3:9, "Where are you?" following Adam and Eve's sin, all through the pages of Scripture to John 21:17, where He asked a humbled Peter, "Do you love Me?" Jesus required people to search their own hearts before they answered Him. Adam hedged his bets while Peter could do little more than admit that he had no impulsive answers left.

In the last four verses of Hebrews chapter 3, the Holy Spirit argues the case for Israel's guilt like an attorney summarizing His case before heaven's jury. He asks three direct "who" questions and then immediately answers them.

Each answer to this triple query points to the same disobedient and rebellious body of people—the nation of Israel. Then in a short statement of fact, He summarizes all that the chapter has described so far in verse 19, "So we see that they were not able to enter [into His rest], because of their unwillingness to adhere to and trust in and rely on God [unbelief had shut them out] (*The Amplified Bible*)."[1] Could God make it any clearer? Trusting in Him and the promises He left us in Scripture leads us into His rest. An unwillingness to place our dependence on those same promises from God shuts us out of His rest. There really are only two choices and Israel repeatedly made the wrong choice!

As chapter 4 begins, the Holy Spirit gives a resounding warning to all believers. By beginning with the word *therefore*, He encompasses in one broad sweep all that He said in the prior chapters—all the warnings, the illustrations, and the quotations from the Old Testament. It's as if He says, "On the basis of all the previous arguments, I want to leave this solemn warning with you." And then our heavenly Father uses a very unusual term. He says we should *fear*. Normally in Scripture, when either the Lord or an angelic being suddenly appeared to people, their first words were, "Fear not!" Yet in the first verse of Hebrews 4 God commands the opposite.

But what is the Holy Spirit telling us to fear or respect? I believe He wants us to make absolutely sure we do not fail to enter into His supernatural rest. Even though we are saved eternally, we could be constantly pulling back through stubbornness or pride and miss the best that God has for us here on earth. You may be thinking, "Well, it may sound childishly simple to you but when I am up at 5:30 in the morning getting three kids out of bed for school, who appear to be in hibernation; making five breakfasts; helping one teenager finish her homework; and locating a gym sock that the dryer appears to have eaten, I am experiencing every emotion but rest." No one can argue with the fact that life's rabid schedule can drain every breath of energy out of us, but God understood that when He wisely warned believers to be on their guard so that they didn't miss out on His rest.

Whenever I read verse 2 of Hebrews chapter 4, I recall a church that I attended many years ago. It was on a main highway but it was a small-town church all the same. It's the only congregation that I've attended where the list of sick people needing prayer was called the *puny list* as in, "Who's on the puny list this week?" This delightful little church comes to mind because I met some friendly people there who had probably been saved for fifty or sixty years, and yet were still *spiritual babies*. They had probably attended this evangelical church since they were in the nursery and now they were crippled with old age. In terms of spiritual discernment, they were childlike. And yet there were others who had been saved in their twenties and were consuming God's Biblical truth like starving teenagers. You could almost see them growing spiritually on a weekly basis. Within a few months' time, they were practicing the truths they had learned and had moved on to more of the meat of the Word.

This paradox bothered me for a long time until I came across chapter 4 and verse 2. It speaks of two groups of believers, both of whom apparently heard the same truth taught from God's Word. What did the first group do that allowed them to enter God's rest and grow, that the latter group failed to do and thus remained unchanged? The answer is at the end of verse 2: "For unto us was the gospel preached, as well as unto them; but the word preached did not profit them, not being mixed with faith in them that heard it."[2] One group that heard the teaching in this friendly little church refused to practice those very principles in their Monday through Saturday lives. They chose not to exercise dependence on God and His Word while they lived and worked in the trenches each week. On Sundays, they camouflaged their real lives with their Sunday lives, making all the right evangelical moves. Year after self-dependent year they continued to sing the choruses of the Cross and attend all the revival services. But after sixty years of near perfect church attendance, there remained a sentence over their lives, "but the word preached did not *profit* them." Saved, but still spiritual babies!

On the other hand, that young twenty-something mother of two who was invited to a ladies Bible study and ran into the love of Christ expressed through those godly prayer warriors, submitted her heart to Christ's Calvary-love. Week after week, she studied God's Word and prayed with older women who were at home in the courts of heaven. Her spiritual growth became visible to everyone! Why? Because all she knew and practiced was to mix *faith* with God's Word as she learned it.

* * * *

When we last mentioned Nancy, Patti, and Tania, they were spending a harried, fearful night along with their children in the Tenenoff's house. Only a few hours earlier, the three husbands and their captors had disappeared into the jungle. Plans were made with Estanislau, a Kuna believer from Pucuro, to take the families down river by means of a large canoe to the nearest Panamanian national town with a two-way radio or a telegraph, and an airstrip. Six a.m. found them on the banks of the Pucuro River with most of the somber-faced Kuna villagers lining the bank. The missionary women loaded the boat with their few belongings and got their children settled on the narrow seats of the dugout. Just minutes earlier, Nancy felt that she should say something as the senior missionary wife to the Kuna gathering. Dave would want that! He had just finished the final Bible lesson in the chronological series leading up to Christ's death, burial, and resurrection, a few days before the kidnapping. Nancy went back over the Biblical gospel message for the benefit of the Kuna villagers present, in their own heart language. She finished by saying, "You have had the opportunity to hear the message that God wanted you to hear. Now it is up to you!"[3] The missionary wives waved tearfully to their dear Kuna friends, and they were on their way. The little group of mothers and children arrived without incident at the frontier town of Boca de Cupe, where they were able to call the mission office in Chame and the U.S. Embassy in Panama City. Not wanting to spend the night there, they continued downriver to the larger town of El Real which had an airstrip. Our mission pilot met them there and transported the emotionally weary little company of wives and children to Panama City. By the end of the day on February 1, 1993, the news of the kidnapping was undoubtedly around the world as an international incident.

My purpose is not to chronicle the events of the vicious kidnapping of three godly missionary men. This has already been very capably documented by Nancy (Mankins) Hamm in her excellent book, *Hostage*.[4] I would rather focus on the topic of God's rest because I have seen this Scriptural principle take on flesh and bones. Following the kidnappings, I observed these three women deal on a daily basis with the uncertainty of their husbands' condition. Sometimes encouraging news was reported from the U.S. Embassy in Panama City; from a Kuna believer in the Darien jungle; or from a captured guerrilla in a Colombian jail. The wives would hear that some white men had been spotted from a distance traveling with a guerrilla troop. Maybe the whole group would be captured by the Colombian military and their husbands would be on the next plane out of Bogota and headed for home. Then they would hear from another incarcerated Colombian guerrilla that he had personally heard that some *gringos* had been buried following a gun battle between guerrillas and the Colombian military. Year after heart-rending year went by, best described as exhilarating highs followed by faith-shattering lows. This was the daily experience of Nancy, Patti, and Tania for almost *nine years*. Even though the three men's bodies were never located, there were numerous reports of their deaths that corroborated each other. It was ultimately agreed by the immediate families to formally and legally declare the men as dead and to hold a memorial service in their honor. On October 6, 2001, a very sacred and meaningful service was held in a church in Longwood, Florida to mark the addition of three more names to the martyrs roll in heaven.

What thoughts do these three missionary wives have about the Biblical subject of God's rest? They experienced virtually every human emotion during those eight plus years of waiting for news. Do they remember experiencing any specific kind of infusion of God's strength? We have spoken of abiding in Christ and His life flowing through us as we exercise faith in Him. Can the three wives honestly say that God walked them through those long dark years with some kind of perceptible help? Or is God's rest only experienced theologically and intellectually?

I asked the three widows, Nancy, Patti, and Tania, five questions very similar to those above and wrote their answers here as direct quotes. I asked the same questions of Gracia Burnham, an NTM missionary widow who served in the Philippines and who also lost her husband to guerrillas there. Gracia's poignant answers are also included in the following chapters.

Let me share with you a few choice thoughts before closing this chapter. Nancy wrote,

"I clearly remember the first few days after Dave, Rick, and Mark were kidnapped, when the thought kept ringing in my ears, 'From the view of eternity, this is going to be all right.' That thought brought spiritual rest to my heart. I knew that God had a plan and that He was in control, so I felt peace in my heart that even though I could not understand, I didn't have to. Unfortunately, without realizing it, I had put a time frame on God's plan. Even though I initially felt peace that from an eternal perspective, whatever God chose would be all right, I didn't realize that His plan would include *waiting without knowing* for an indefinite period of time. I thought that Dave, Rick, and Mark would be released within a month or so, like other New Tribes missionaries had been. Or even in the worst-case scenario, we would learn that they had been taken home to be with God. But I had not considered the months, much less the years, of not knowing whether they were alive and suffering or in heaven.

"My world came tumbling down and I began to *lose it* spiritually speaking. I was afraid and angry. I was afraid that God was not hearing our prayers and I was angry at God because He could do something and was choosing not to. Once I realized and admitted to myself that I was angry with God, I was able to deal with it by reading the Bible and choosing to believe the passages that tell me that God loves me. He is compassionate; He is able; and He does hear my prayers. The kidnappers took away my husband and my ministry but they could not take away my ability to choose *joy* as I walked through this trial. I had to daily, sometimes hourly, choose to focus on God. I had to choose to read God's Word and believe that God's Word is true. I had to choose to pray and choose God's will over my own. Often at night, I would find that my hands were clenched into fists and I would have to literally pry them open as I prayed for the ability to relinquish my husband again to God and His will."

Patti shared some helpful thoughts concerning the role that our *minds* play in entering consistently into God's rest. She said, "I know that you have heard the expression, 'the mind is the battlefield.' One time I threw a hard-boiled egg across the room that I could not seem to peel properly. Then I cried; I yelled at God; I sat on the floor; I cried some more; and I told God what I was thinking in my heart. As I listened to myself expressing my thoughts to God, I recognized the untruthfulness of them. I had been listening to Satan's lies. So I would often turn back to God's Word and remind myself of what I knew was truth. I tried to focus on God instead of myself and remember that God was looking at the big picture."

CHAPTER TEN – THEMES FOR FURTHER STUDY

- The book of Hebrews describes another privilege for Christians who choose God's rest—they become actual "partakers of Christ". (Hebrews 3:14)

- God's rest is so important to Him that He urges His children to *fear* or give high importance to the fact that some believers could possibly "come short of it". (Hebrews 4:1)

- Two groups of believers can hear the same Biblical teaching—one group will grow rapidly in their knowledge of Christ while the other group remains spiritually immature. Why? The first group exercised faith in God and His Word and chose to live a life of spiritual rest—the other rejected His rest and therefore God's Word "did not profit them". (Hebrews 4:2)

Chapter 11

RESTING SOUNDS GOOD— BUT HOW DOES IT WORK?

I haven't wanted this to be a how-to book, as in *Seven No-Fail Steps to Entering into God's Rest*. As I explained to someone in a recent letter, "My goal in writing on this subject is to present the various Bible verses where God describes this wonderful mystery that He calls My rest, and then to sprinkle in between these verses real life experiences of my own and of other believers, where the Lord made His strength and care very evident. Walking with the Lord under the control of His Spirit can be *messy*, from our point of view at least—certainly not from God's. In other words, our experience of God's rest is not just neat, sterile, and made to fit into precise little sanctified slots. To me, the wonder of His rest is that our imperfect experience of that rest doesn't take a single thing away from His awesome care for us."

Tania (Rich) Julin explains this very principle in practical terms in her following testimony:

> "To me it didn't feel, at the time, like spiritual rest. It felt more like a battle and God was giving me strength to stand firm and be a good soldier on the

actual night of the kidnapping. The choice to believe that God is who He says He is, and not choose to base my joy and peace on the feelings I was experiencing, was what it boiled down to for me. It is hard to relinquish what I feel is only fair and right for me to experience in my life. I didn't feel like I was asking for too much and yet I was stubbornly demanding that my life turn around and start going the way I wanted it to go. It was only when I gave up completely my hopes and dreams for my life and my future that I would sense God's peace and love and joy flowing freely again.

"It is hard to explain but it wasn't giving up in a defeated sort of way—it was in a sweet way saying to God, 'I trust You more than I trust what feels good to me right now and I sincerely believe that You have *good* planned for me through this situation.' It was not a ceasing to care or disengagement—it was a deep sense of giving up what felt vital to my well-being, in order to take hold of something bigger, deeper, and better than what I thought I wanted. I believe it was C. S. Lewis who talked about being content making mud pies when the seashore is just over the hill. The last part of this cycle takes time for me to really grab hold of. It was and still is through quiet times with God and His Word that this rest could come.

"I think it was the realization that David, who wrote so many of the Psalms, was called by God 'a man after God's own heart' and that the apostles Paul and Peter were greatly used by God in spite of times of intense questioning and doubting. I was able to take courage that God was still going to use me and wasn't necessarily punishing me or unhappy with me in some way. There were periods of time when I couldn't seem to understand anything that I read in the Bible—it felt cold and unintelligible. I learned to be okay with those times and keep reading—to ask God to help me to be able to understand again and He always did. The Bible is not some magic potion that you read and then your circumstances are going to seem okay all of a sudden. It is full of stories of God and His strength and wisdom and power. I read it and was encouraged; I read it and was confused; I read it and got frustrated; but in the end, reading the Bible caused me to ask God for help in understanding and applying what I had read."

God tells us throughout Hebrews 3 and 4, that in order for believers to enter His rest, we have to make certain choices. I would like us to look at three other New Testament verses that deal with both what we are responsible to do—choose to exercise trust in the person of God Himself and His Word—and what God is responsible to do; provide us with His divine rest. These following three verses seem to fill in details around those we have already looked at concerning His rest. They make a solid wall of truth that will support us throughout our lives:

Galatians 2:20–Indwelling
2 Peter 1:3-4–Transforming
1 John 1:9–Confessing

INDWELLING–Galatians 2:20
This verse has been absolutely life-changing for me personally. I love the way *The Amplified Bible* states it, "I have been crucified with Christ [in Him I have shared His crucifixion]; it is no longer I who live, but Christ (the Messiah) lives in me; and the life I now live in the body I live by faith in (by adherence to and reliance on and complete trust in) the Son of God, Who loved me and gave Himself up for me."[1]

From the moment that I first trusted in Jesus' death on the cross and He became my Savior, a long list of divine blessings took place in my life and I was oblivious to most of them. One of those blessings, according to this verse, is that the unregenerate person that I was before salvation actually died on the cross along with Jesus—not to bear anyone's sin like Jesus did, but so that God could put Christ's resurrection life within me in place of my own sinful self. Yes, I still sin as a child of God, but since the time of my salvation, Galatians 2:20 says that I have the very person of the Son of God living within me, whereas before salvation, Scripture says that I was God's *enemy*.

Ian Thomas states this truth so eloquently: "To be *in Christ*—that is redemption; but for Christ to be *in you*—that is sanctification! To be *in Christ*—that makes you fit for heaven; but for Christ to be *in you*—that makes you fit for earth! To be *in Christ*—that changes your destination; but for Christ to be *in you*—that changes your destiny! The one makes heaven your home—the other makes this world His workshop."[2]

Verse 20 says that since we shared Christ's crucifixion with Him, "It is no longer I who live, but Christ lives in me." Isn't that thrilling beyond words? We simply place our trust in God's Son and besides God forgiving all of our past and future sin, the Bible says that the Creator of the universe, Jesus Christ, takes up His residence inside of us. Here is the part of the verse that eliminated for me so much of the self-effort to please God: "And the life which I now live in the flesh I *live by faith* (emphasis added)." Faith must have a target—an object toward which the trust is directed. Notice the synonyms for *faith* in *The Amplified Bible's* rendering of this verse, "by faith in (by adherence to and reliance on and complete trust in) the Son of God, Who loved me and gave Himself up for me."[3]

Ian Thomas clearly describes the dual truth of Christ doing it all (passive on our part) and our exercising faith (active on our part): "As far as God is concerned, Christ is the preacher, Christ is the missionary, Christ is the Christian worker, Christ is the witnessing Christian. Only what *He* is, and what *He* does, is righteousness—and what He is, and what He does, is only released through you by your unrelenting attitude of dependence. This is called faith—and 'whatsoever is not of faith is sin' (Romans 14:23c)."[4] What an indescribable gift! We depend on Jesus to live the only life through us that He is capable of living—His life. And that is why God calls this supernatural relationship His rest.

TRANSFORMING–2 Peter 1:3-4

It was mentioned earlier that the word *transformed*, used in 2 Corinthians 3:18 to express this principle of the believer being spiritually changed, is undoubtedly where we got our English word *metamorphosis*. In a limited sense, we see the same picture of our transformation into Christ's image as we see in the complete metamorphosis of the Monarch butterfly—first a plain egg; then a brightly striped caterpillar; next a chrysalis; and finally the stunningly bronzed adult. In both cases, it is wholly an act of our very creative God!

Before the Lord explains, through the apostle Peter, that we believers are sharers in His divine nature, He makes a singular promise to His children that ought to satisfy every longing we could ever have. That promise is not followed by a list of qualifications and subcategories but rather God states uncompromisingly, "Seeing that His divine power has granted to us *everything* pertaining to life and godliness (emphasis added)" (2 Peter 1:3). Can you think of any area of your daily life that falls outside of this promise? Is there any significant aspect of what you will ever face between now and your graduation day into heaven that would extend beyond the limits of "everything that pertains to life and godliness?" So, if those are the parameters for the rest of our lives, including the worst nightmare that we may ever have to face, surely God has us covered with His divine *everything*.

What is the key that unlocks this supernatural storehouse of provision which God promises to turn inside out for us according to our needs and His will? The apostle Peter declares that it is through the true knowledge of Him. There is that expression again—*knowing Christ*! Is it any wonder then that Moses, beholding God in His righteous anger in the wilderness, would come up with the surprisingly simple request, "Let me know Thy ways, that I may know Thee" (Exodus 33:13). Did God, who had been previously talking to Moses about Israel's willful disobedience, say to Moses, "Moses, please try and stay focused on what we are discussing"? No! God seemed to rejoice over Moses' mature discernment and He exultingly replied in the following verse, "My presence shall go with you, and I will give you rest." By that response, surely God was saying, "That's it, Moses! You have hit on what is truly important. As you enter into My rest, you will come to know Me. And through knowing Me, all of the promises that I make to you will be a reality."

Several thousand years later, the apostle Paul distilled his years of sacrificial devotion and service to the Lord Jesus into the closest thing to a formula for victorious Christian living that we ever hear from Paul. In Philippians 3:8 he writes, "I count all things to be loss in view of the surpassing value of knowing Christ Jesus my Lord." Two verses later, Paul said simply, "that I may know Him."

Let's return to Chapter 1 of Second Peter. When we read in verse 4 that His promises are *precious* and *magnificent*, we can be confident of their immeasurable worth. Here we read from the pen of Peter that it is through exercising faith (by implication) in God's promises that little by little we begin to look just like Jesus. We have become "partakers of the divine nature" or, as we read earlier, "for we have become partakers of Christ" (Hebrews 3:14).

CONFESSING–1 John 1:9

Why include a verse that talks about us being disobedient to God and rebellious against His Word? After all, we have been reading glorious truths about Christ living in us; Jesus living out His perfect life through our daily lives; and how Christians abiding in God's rest undergo a spiritual metamorphosis. Why talk, then, about confession and forgiveness of sin? It must be included here because the issue of unconfessed, and therefore unforgiven sin, is probably the principle reason Christians can hear frequent teaching on God's rest and yet not change one smidgen. Believers understand that because of their trust in Christ's death on the cross of Calvary, their sin—past, present, and future—is entirely paid for. God the Father sees each of His redeemed children only in the perfection of His divine Son, Jesus—*never* apart from Him.

This is not the sin that is in view in the first epistle of John. Rather it is those daily demonstrations of our own independence. It is our decision to make our own choices rather than choose what we know God wants. It's the fruit of our angry outbursts or our unwillingness to let go of a hurt in order to forgive someone. King Solomon, in the Old Testament, wisely talks about "the little foxes that are ruining the vineyards" (The Song of Solomon 2:15). No, God will not send a believer to hell for having an angry attitude, because Christ has already paid the consequences of that believer's sin. Besides the angry remark wounding the hearer, it has a far more serious consequence. It has broken *fellowship* between the angry Christian and the Lord Jesus. Between the time that the believer sinned and then confessed that sin to God, a break in *relationship* occurred, not a break in the believer's *eternal standing* with God.

At the moment of our salvation, the Holy Spirit takes up residence in us. Within our hearts, the Spirit not only lives out the life of Jesus through us, but He also brings to our attention occasions when we sin against God. Sometimes I sense His nudges even while I am being tempted and before I actually commit the sin. That is His ministry—after all, we now belong to the heavenly Father. What if we ignore His prompting and give way to the anger welling up inside us? In my own case, I usually know it right away—it's like I just drove through a stop sign. Almost immediately I sense God prompting me to admit to myself and then to Him that I chose self over God's will. Our relationship is now disjointed—like a limb out of joint. I am no longer enjoying uninterrupted fellowship—I'm not resting with my Savior. Saved? Yes! In a right relationship with Jesus Christ? Definitely not!

At times like this we can justify ourselves and rationalize why we had a right to be angry. We tell ourselves that we were acting appropriately to the situation. But down deep in our souls we sense that almost imperceptible voice of the Holy Spirit saying, "You have chosen your own path over mine!" There really are only two courses of action at this point. We can stubbornly refuse to admit that we did anything wrong. We then experience inner turmoil since the Holy Spirit is constantly reminding us of our sin and we are constantly excusing our wrong behavior in our minds. In this state, we cannot enter into God's rest. There is definitely a *lack of peace* in our hearts since peace comes from communion with Jesus Christ. We are unhappy since *joy* is also a part of the fruit of the Spirit. We don't laugh much because there doesn't seem to be very much in life that is humorous. And so we become increasingly miserable and touchy. In addition, we stop growing spiritually and as the book of Hebrews says in *The Amplified Bible*, "For even though by this time you ought to be teaching others, you actually need someone to teach you over again the very first principles of

God's Word. You have come to need milk, not solid food" (Hebrews 5:12).[5]

Our other choice is to allow the Holy Spirit to explain to our heart and mind why our act of anger was sin; instead of arguing defensively, we can admit that He is right. In so doing, the fruit of the Spirit—the personality of Jesus Christ—is once again operational in our lives. The apostle Paul explained that Jesus Christ "manifests through us the sweet aroma of the knowledge of Him in every place" (2 Corinthians 2:14). In addition to these blessings from the Father, we grow spiritually and gradually become conformed to the image of Christ. This is God's rest!

The first epistle of John states clearly that believers are not perfect but will occasionally sin until we receive our perfect heavenly bodies. It reads, "If we say that we have no sin, we are deceiving ourselves, and the truth is not in us" (1 John 1:8). But then God's precious promise declares, "If we confess our sins, He is faithful and righteous to forgive us our sins and to cleanse us from *all* unrighteousness (emphasis added)" (I John 1:9). Can you believe how simple God has made it? All that He asks of His children when they sin is that they honestly admit it to Him. No slavish groveling! No paying money! No promising to never do it again! It doesn't even say in the verse that we have to tell God we are sorry—He knows our *true* feelings. Are you ready for this? The verse of Scripture doesn't even say that we have to ask God to forgive us. That is God's promise in response to our confession of sin to Him and Him alone. Men through the centuries have refused to accept the simplicity of God's promise in John's first letter and have wanted to add human works to try and partly pay for their transgression. When we sin, only God can say, "I forgive you" in response to our honest admission. If it is by grace then it has to be all God!

CHAPTER ELEVEN – THEMES FOR FURTHER STUDY

- Three more Bible verses that complement the topic of God's rest are:

- *Galatians 2:20* – As a believer, I have Jesus Christ residing in me through the Holy Spirit, willing and capable to do all that pleases God through me.

- *2 Peter 1:3-4* – Not only has God given me "everything pertaining to life and godliness," but by faith I become an actual *partaker* of Christ.

- *1 John 1:9* – When I sin as a Christian, and until I confess it and am forgiven, my *relationship* with Jesus Christ is hindered, not my *standing*. As soon as I admit the sin to God, He forgives me and cleanses me from "all unrighteousness."

Chapter 12

CHRIST IN YOU, THE HOPE OF GLORY

In her outstanding book, *In The Presence of My Enemies,* Gracia Burnham recounts how she and her husband Martin were kidnapped on May 27, 2001, by Abu Sayyaf guerrillas, while they celebrated their wedding anniversary on the Philippine Island of Palawan. The Burnhams and fifteen other captives, including one other American man, were ordered from their Dos Palmas hotel rooms at gun point during the night and literally herded into a waiting speedboat. The captives were transported by various boats across the Sulu Sea to the primarily Muslim island called Basilan. For the next year, Martin and Gracia tramped all over this island with a ragged troop of nominally Islamic guerrillas, led by the charismatic Abu Sabaya. This saga ended in wave after wave of gunfire on June 7, 2002, as the guerrillas and their captives rested in their hammocks. The Philippine military, who tracked this little party for the entire year, had finally caught up with them and when the automatic weapons were silent, Martin Burnham lay dead on the ground with bullet wounds to his chest, and next to him lay his beloved wife Gracia, a bullet piercing her leg.

Rather than recount further details of the Burnham's story, I will instead refer you to Gracia's own compelling autobiography. For our purposes in looking at the subject of God's rest, it would be more helpful to learn how God reached out to this couple during their year of captivity in the jungle—to hear from Gracia concerning His rest. In other words, it's clear and simple in theory, but how did it work during one of the most gripping missionary dramas of this century?

Having looked at considerable Scripture concerning the topic of God's rest, we might well ask, "This principle probably worked like a charm for Christ's disciples and other Biblical giants but how about *my* life, which in comparison would rate as pretty mundane?" The answer to that query is the very reason I would like for us to hear from Gracia and the three ladies I introduced earlier. They were housewives and mothers even before they were missionaries working in third world countries. God chose to allow these dear women to go through excruciating emotional times that we rarely read about. Did God honestly come through with His rest? How did *His Word* help, when no amount of human comfort was adequate? What did they learn about *prayer* during the intensity of the spiritual warfare? How did the high drama help them come to *know Him* better? Which of Christ's characteristics became most precious to them?

As I read over Gracia's answers to these questions, I thought that the subject of God's rest could be best served by letting you hear from Gracia herself.

Were there any intense occasions in particular where you experienced God's restful presence and an awareness that He was still in control of the situation?

GRACIA – At one point, about a month into our captivity, we had been in a gun battle and were fleeing the area. At one rest stop, I went off to use the bathroom and as I stepped back on the trail, everyone was moving out (we tended to hike all night to get out of areas that we knew the military was in). I fell in line behind Martin and a ways down the trail, realized that I had left our backpack with *all* of our stuff back where I had gone to the bathroom. I turned around to retrieve it and they wouldn't let me go back. I lost everything we owned! It was clearly my fault and I was sobbing as I followed Martin down the trail asking him to forgive me for losing all our possessions. There wasn't much—but they were so important!

There had been a sheet I had gotten at a hospital where we had been a few days before; a toothbrush that we were sharing; some underwear, a shirt—what were we going to do without that sheet to keep us warm at night? I was so broken up that I had made such a stupid mistake! Martin at one point turned and said to me, "Gracia, I forgive you—now you need to forgive yourself." That really struck a chord with me. He always seemed to know what to say to me.

Anyway, the next day we got to a little Muslim village and the villagers killed a cow so we had plenty to eat. And that very day, a Muslim woman dressed all in black came into that village with a big box from our NTM Headquarters in Manila. How did she know we would be there? I'll never know. But in that box was everything that I had just left behind the night before—plus extra stuff—and letters from our kids telling us that they were in America and they were okay. I am sure there could be a logical explanation—one of the guys got on the cell phone and arranged that the box come in, or whatever, but I believe it was God wanting me to know that He was bigger than any mistake I could make; that He was going to take care of us. We ended up running from that village too, when the military found us—but what a great lesson I took away from that experience—that I could trust God to take care of things in the future because He was able to do it in the past.

Would you describe this time as a time of "spiritual rest"?

I surely would! We gave all the glory to God that afternoon. We prayed and thanked God for this huge *reminder* that He was in control and we again put our trust in Him to get us through another day.

What helped you most when you found that you were "losing it" spiritually, in order to enter back into God's rest?

GRACIA – God's Word is what helped us the most. Often when we were discouraged and we didn't know how to encourage each other any more because we had no more encouraging words, we would sit and quote Scripture to one another. Martin would even say, "Let's sit here and remind ourselves of what is true." And we would quote, "If God be for us, who can be against us?" "I have loved you with an everlasting love." "You have been blessed with every spiritual blessing in the heavenlies." At that particular time, we didn't *feel* blessed. We didn't *feel* loved. We didn't *feel* that God was even necessarily for us. So we pushed our feelings aside and reminded ourselves—again—of what was true. "I have called you by My name—you are Mine." "When you go through the floods, I will be with you." We chose to believe that God's Word is true and that it applied to us even if we didn't feel that way. The only thing that could comfort us in those times was God's Word.

What attribute or characteristic of Christ's nature provided you the most comfort?

GRACIA – What brought me comfort was knowing that He loves me. I reaffirmed that belief about ten weeks into our captivity. For a few days, I decided that, contrary to what I was taught, God must not love me because He wasn't coming through for me. That led to despair, depression, and being irritable. After a few days of wrestling with that, I decided to believe what the Scripture says, that God loves me so He was *not* going to forsake a creature that He loved.

How did you go about applying Scripture to your life during the darkest moments?

GRACIA – The times that Scripture was the most precious were the times that it would just pop into my head when I needed it most. I remember one day we had hiked for days and nights to get out of a critical area and we were hiking up yet another mountain. I had a backpack, two mortars (one in each hand), and was exhausted, and the verses from Hebrews 12 came to mind. "Seeing that we are surrounded by this cloud of witnesses, let us lay aside every weight [the things that exhaust us as we are climbing] and the sin that so easily besets us [discouragement in this case] and let us run with patience the race that is set before us [this extreme situation that I found myself in that I couldn't get free from was my race at the time]. Looking unto Jesus, the author and finisher of our faith, who for the joy that was set before Him endured the cross, despising the shame, and is set down at the right hand of God." Too bad I didn't remember the rest of that section about how Christ didn't give up when sinful people did such terrible things to Him; and the encouragement that we hadn't yet given our lives in this struggle, at least.

*   *   *   *

It would be a shame to conclude this book without looking at the verses that gave us the title—Mark 6:31-32. They thrill me every time I read them because they demonstrate in such a clear and simple fashion how sensitive Jesus

Christ is to how I feel—that it is human to be exhausted physically and emotionally, and He understands. He is actually in favor of me taking time to build myself back up when I am *out of energy*, even as a result of Christian service. Throughout this book, we have looked at the *spiritual* side of God's rest because it is primarily a spiritual condition. Before finishing, however, I would like to look briefly at the *physical* side, since the Lord obviously addressed it in the book of Mark. These two verses speak primarily of balancing our busy lives with adequate physical rest—in other words, the *physical* side of God's rest.

I believe that the Christian who walks consistently under the control of the Holy Spirit—confessing all known sin on a regular basis as the Holy Spirit convicts them—will experience a great measure of physical and emotional stability. However, the tendency of many is to live frantically, because we schedule our days and evenings beyond full. Unfortunately, we can be driven more by a desire to please other people than to please God. We say, "Sure I'd be happy to do that!" instead of stopping for even a nanosecond and praying, "Father, is this something that You want me to do?" Jesus never overcommitted Himself during His relatively short life on earth. Why? Because His heart and mind were constantly inquiring what His Father's will was.

You could say, "Well, even if I did stop and pray before committing to another appointment, could I expect to hear a clear *Yes* or *No* in my mind?" The Epistle of James indicates that the Lord is well able to communicate His heart's desire to us. We read, "But if any of you lacks wisdom, let him ask of God, who gives to all men generously and without reproach, and it will be given to him" (James 1:5). God intended that the norm for His children was to choose by faith to *abide* in Him (John 15). Hebrews 3 and 4 describes this relationship as entering into *God's rest*. The first epistle of John declares, that we should *walk in fellowship with Him*. It is a spiritually restful condition that is accompanied by a physical rest as well.

I don't believe God ever intended Christians to so fill their calendars with stressful commitments that they have the same percentage of emotional breakdowns as unbelievers. Life is full of unavoidable pressure and the Lord Jesus wants to walk us through these tough areas assured of His presence within us. Often, it's the 120 percent overload that we independently choose to pack into our already full lives that pushes us over the edge. God in His grace and lovingkindness will often absorb the ill effects of that—for a while. But if we continue to ignore the Holy Spirit's voice telling us things like, "Slow down a minute here and let's discuss whether I really want you to agree to join that committee that you are considering," it will eventually cost us.

Therefore, I believe that God's *spiritual* rest is accompanied by a *physical* peace and tranquility of body, mind, and emotions. Unfortunately, many in the body of Christ are probably not experiencing that tranquility of soul on a consistent basis but suffer from the same degree of stress, high blood pressure, and panic attacks as those who do not know Christ.

The Lord Jesus seems to have sensed this same stressful weariness in His disciples in Mark 6:31. He chose to exhort them and us! Let's look at each encouraging phrase:

HE (JESUS) SAID – I draw great encouragement from the fact that the Lord Jesus Himself acknowledged that His disciples were in overload following their missionary venture and He was giving them permission to rest and get refreshed. Because I have decided to follow the Lord and to serve Him at His pleasure, I've noticed my tendency to say, "Yes, I would be glad to" instead of, "I would really like to pray about it first" and then follow through and pray. It's a subtle thing that coaxes you to think that doing more Christian service is always better, compared with simply walking under the Holy Spirit's direction moment by moment.

COME AWAY – Isn't that a comforting invitation, especially since Jesus said it? I can picture the expression on the Lord's face as He looked at His worn out disciples. He probably beckoned with His hand to His devoted followers as He said, "I know that you are all excited about what you did on your recent ministry trip, but I can discern that all of you are worn out. Let's find a quiet place where we can talk and rest and you can share with Me all that you have experienced recently. I can't wait to hear it!"

BY YOURSELVES – We are all wired differently. Some people seem to need people around them all the time as if their batteries are recharged from the energy of others. We also know people who prefer long periods of solitude and are agitated the whole time they have to be with others. Most of us fall between these two extremes, but in this instance Jesus seems to be saying, "This is the time for solitude and rest. For a short while I want us to block out the rest of the world to give you time to pray by yourself, pray as groups, sleep, read, and generally replenish yourselves."

TO A LONELY PLACE – Do you regularly schedule into your calendar a time to be in a lonely place of refreshing? There is no question that it has to be well planned for, because most of us will always opt for the people and responsibilities that tug at us. We must first be convinced that God not only approves of us taking time for refreshing but He urges us to, knowing how He made us. My normal reaction is to feel *guilt* at even considering some private renewal time. Could I actually be disobeying the Holy Spirit's voice within me?

AND REST A WHILE – Much has been discussed and written in recent years concerning *Sabbath rest*. Since it refers to an aspect of the nature of God Himself, the term can be found throughout Scripture as a literal day. It first appears in reference to the days of creation and also to the special relationship between God and the nation of Israel. In the New Testament, where we find instruction for the church and the body of Christ, reference to the Sabbath rest appears to be used in a more figurative or spiritual sense.

Genesis 2:2–"And by the seventh day God completed His work which He had done; and He rested on the seventh day from all His work which He had done." Why would God take a full day to rest after six days of creation? Obviously He was not worn out, even though you and I might look at the enormity of the universe and think that He had every right to be. I believe, as do many others, that by God including a final day where He created nothing along with six days of active creation, He was demonstrating that He had finished and completed all He had started out to do. All that God planned to create from the beginning of time, He chose to do in six days and He punctuated the end of this creative omnipotence with a day characterized by rest. What He made in six days was perfect and required no extra time for repairs or tweaking. We will see the application to the Christian life later in the book of Hebrews.

Deuteronomy 5:12-15–"Observe the sabbath day to keep it holy, as the Lord your God commanded you. Six days you shall labor and do all your work, but the seventh day is a sabbath of the Lord your God; in it you shall not do any work, you or your son or your daughter or your male servant or your female servant or your ox or your donkey or any of your cattle or your sojourner who stays with you, so that your male servant and your female servant may rest as well as you. And you shall remember that you were a slave in the land of Egypt, and the Lord your God brought you out of there by a mighty hand and by an outstretched arm; therefore the Lord your God commanded you to observe the sabbath day." God, in His relationship with the nation of Israel, placed a very special importance on the Sabbath. It was the fourth commandment of the ten and God defined very carefully for Israel how He wanted it to be observed. There were primarily two aspects to Sabbath observance—not doing any work on the seventh day of the week and also *remembering*. In the first instance, a Jewish person's immediate family, their animals, their servants, and even their visitors, were commanded not to work on the Sabbath day. Verse 15 makes it clear that each Sabbath, all of Israel was to remember how their God had taken them out of slavery in Egypt by the power of His might. It was to be a *memorial*!

Ezekiel 20: 12, 13–"And also I gave them My sabbaths to be a sign between Me and them, that they might know that I am the Lord who sanctifies them. But the house of Israel rebelled against Me in the wilderness. They did not walk in My statutes, and they rejected My ordinances, by which, if a man observes them, he will live; and My sabbaths they greatly profaned. Then I resolved to pour out My wrath on them in the wilderness, to annihilate them."

During the time of Israel's history in the Old Testament, God chose for the Sabbath to be a sign that was specifically between Himself and His covenant people Israel.

Hebrews 4:3-11–"For we who have believed enter that rest, just as He has said, 'As I swore in My wrath, they shall not enter My rest,' although His works were finished from the foundation of the world. For He has thus said somewhere concerning the seventh day, 'And God rested on the seventh day from all His works'; and again in this passage, 'They shall not enter My rest.' Since therefore it remains for some to enter it, and those who formerly had good news preached to them failed to enter because of disobedience,

He again fixes a certain day, 'Today,' saying through David after so long a time just as has been said before, 'Today if you hear His voice, do not harden your hearts.' For if Joshua had given them rest, He would not have spoken of another day after that. There remains therefore a Sabbath rest for the people of God. For the one who has entered His rest has himself also rested from his works, as God did from His. Let us therefore be diligent to enter that rest, lest anyone fall through following the same example of disobedience." For the Christian believer and member of the body of Christ, the teaching of these verses is truly *awe inspiring*. As we read earlier in chapter 3 of Hebrews, the Lord had been describing how Israel failed to enter by faith into God's rest. Christians are exhorted that, "today" we should be sure not to *harden our hearts* nor *fail to enter God's rest*. Remember how in the Genesis account of creation that the seventh day of noncreativity spoke of God's completion of all that He desired to create. Now, in the church teaching of the book of Hebrews, God refers back to His completed acts of creation to include—are *you ready for this?*—His rest! Hebrews 4:3 says, "For we who have *believed* enter that rest." Now look at verse 9 of chapter 4. It reads, "There remains therefore a Sabbath rest for the people of God." Is this speaking of the nation of Israel? No, because the context up to this point in Hebrews has been *believers*, true children of God through faith in Jesus Christ.

Verse 10 continues to speak of believers resting from their works, just like God rested from His works on the seventh day. God instructs us that the rest He offers us is a part of Him and His nature—the very presence and being of Jesus Christ—and therefore has existed from eternity past as He has. God seems to be telling His children, "Stop trying to bring about spiritual growth through your own efforts. Stop trying to follow Christ's example through your own strength. Get off the treadmill of dead, lifeless works—they cannot *save* you just like they cannot *mature* you. I have provided everything you will ever need for salvation as well as everything you'll need for Christian growth. And both are in and through the person of the Son of God, Jesus Christ." How do we enter that restful place of intimacy with God? Only by faith! And faith involves us setting aside our own futile works and resting (literally relaxing) in God's completed sufficiency.

Verse 11 sounds like a paradox. The KJV states it, "Let us *labor*, therefore, to enter into that *rest*."[1] Because of what has been stated in earlier chapters, we know that it does *not* mean that we should try in our own laborious efforts to enter God's rest. I believe it means, "Be zealous! Be diligent! Whatever you do, make sure that you don't overlook resting in Jesus Christ." Is it any wonder that verse 12 would explain the power of the Word of God since we claim the surety of God's rest through the promises that He has left us in His precious Word?

How does all of the above apply to Christ's exhortation to His disciples to get away and be refreshed physically? The Lord who designed and formed us knows better than anyone that we cannot remain healthy physically, emotionally, and spiritually without adequate time away from our work. We need to set the aggravations and weariness of work aside and give our bodies, minds, and spirits an opportunity to focus on other meaningful areas of our lives—worshipping our Savior individually and corporately in the local church; developing meaningful relationships with our spouse, our children, and others; napping; exercising; reading. We need to break the 24/7 grip that work can have on us in order to develop the other meaningful areas of our lives. So much of the Spirit-controlled life can best be described by the word *balance*.

FOR THERE WERE MANY PEOPLE COMING AND GOING, AND THEY DID NOT EVEN HAVE TIME TO EAT - Does this not sound strangely similar to our current frenetic lifestyle in America?

CHAPTER TWELVE –THEMES FOR FURTHER STUDY

- Gracia had a great deal of difficulty forgiving herself for leaving her backpack behind. Can you think of a time when you had trouble forgiving yourself even though you had admitted it to the Lord and knew He forgave you? What more could you have done to remedy your feelings?

- What sound advice did Martin give when the Burnhams were discouraged and had no more encouraging words? Why is that principle the "road out of discouragement"? What do we often do in times of discouragement that undermines this principle?

- Have you ever considered the practical consequences of God's love for you?

- Would you say that we are more likely to be at rest physically and emotionally if we are at rest spiritually? Is that your experience?

- Is part of the reason for your daily schedule being *frantic*—if that is the case—a desire to please other people rather than consult the Lord?

- Would you agree that the Holy Spirit wants to be the keeper of your time schedule and that He will not over schedule you? Does He put up warning signs when you over commit yourself?

- Why didn't Jesus suffer from burnout and overload when He walked this earth? (Hebrews 4:15 says that Jesus experienced all the same temptations that we do, without sinning.)

- What is it about quiet times of solitude that is so refreshing? Could busyness and noise steal from our intimacy with Jesus Christ?

- Is it realistic for you to plan times of quiet reflection, prayer, Bible study, and worship into your yearly schedule?

- Explain why God planned a Sabbath rest day following six very creative days.

- Why do you think God was so determined that Israel should obey a Sabbath rest day?

- It sounds like an oxymoron for God to urge Christians to be diligent or labor to enter into God's rest. What does it actually mean? (Hebrew 4:11)

Chapter 13

FINDING GOD'S REST IN THE FURNACE OF TRIAL

Wouldn't it be awesome if the moment we become Christian believers, the Lord Jesus excused us from any further suffering? Or maybe it wouldn't be so great. God is very clear in His Word in telling His children that they can *count on* suffering in this life. The apostle Paul wrote in the book of Romans, "Only we must share His suffering if we are to share His glory. [But what of that?] For I consider that the sufferings of this present time (this present life) are not worth being compared with the glory that is about to be revealed to us and in us and for us and conferred on us! (*The Amplified Bible*)" (Romans 8:17(b)–18).[1]

None of us enjoys suffering. But what a comfort that if we share Christ's suffering now, in this life, that we will also share in His divine glory when we are in heaven. Furthermore, while we are experiencing the *furnace of trial*, we have His word that He will be right there with us also. I love the picture Moses drew in his final words to Israel, before his death: "The eternal God is a dwelling place, and underneath are the everlasting arms" (Deuteronomy 33:27).

When we think of the word *furnace*, there is usually one Old Testament story that comes to mind—that of Shadrach, Meshach and Abednego. You remember that these three young Hebrew men, along with Daniel and others, had been forcibly removed from Judea and taken to Babylon. Chapter 3 of the book of Daniel tells a very dramatic story while at the same time teaching us that God experiences with us every trial that we face.

This particular saga begins in verses 1-7 with Nebuchadnezzar, King of Babylon, making a decree that at a given signal, every person had to fall down and worship the 90 foot golden statue of the king or be put into a blazing furnace. It's not long before some Chaldeans in Babylon become aware that the three Hebrew youths are not obeying the decree: "These men, O king, have disregarded you; they do not serve your gods or worship the golden image which you have set up" (Daniel 3:12).

The king, in a raging fit, calls the three young men to him and gives them two choices. They are to fall down and worship the image he made or be cast into the blazing furnace. His next statement indicates clearly how his pride had totally distorted his reason. Nebuchadnezzar added, "And what god is there who can deliver you out of my hands?" (Daniel 3:15).

The answer from the three young men is so profound that it has to be looked at phrase by phrase, beginning with verse 17:

- IF IT BE SO – If the worst case scenario does come about, and God does allow us to be put into the furnace, it will only be because that's what He is permitting.
- OUR GOD WHOM WE SERVE – That's the irreducible minimum—we worship and serve the One True God of Israel and no one else—period!

- IS ABLE TO DELIVER US FROM THE FURNACE OF BLAZING FIRE – In other words, there is nothing—no hazard, no danger, no calamity, and no disease—that our God is not able to handle.
- AND HE WILL DELIVER US OUT OF YOUR HAND, O KING - Doesn't that make you want to stand up and cheer? Aren't they saying that whether they go into the furnace or not, they will be under the protection of their heavenly Father—even if it appeared like the king had his way?
- BUT EVEN IF HE DOES NOT – What is the issue here? God's personal will is! Shadrach, Meshach, and Abednego were experiencing *God's rest* and that rest came from the fact that they had fastened every fiber of their being to the will of God. They were confident in the character of God from what they *knew* of Him—from the limited Scriptures available to them at that time and their own experience of God's faithfulness. And that brings rest!

Notice the same principle in Hebrews chapter 11. In verse 34, we read of faithful brethren who "escaped the edge of the sword." Several verses later, we read of other faithful brethren who "were put to death with the sword." What made the difference? The sovereign will of God did!

What is the lesson, then from these three young men of faith, in Daniel chapter 3? It's that God is *able* to deliver me out of the worst of circumstances. But if He doesn't choose to, I can, as His child, rest in His Father-love, knowing what I do about Him, both from Scripture and from what He has personally taught my heart. Will I choose to be content with *His choices*?

* * * *

I shared in an earlier chapter of this book, the story of the actual kidnapping of the three missionary men, by F.A.R.C. guerrillas, from the Kuna Indian village of Pucuro in the Darien jungle of Panama. The wives and children made it out of the jungle on February 1, 1993—the day following the actual kidnapping. With the help of the U.S. Embassy personnel, NTM set up a crisis center that same day, in our mission pilot's house in Panama City. Three NTM leadership couples lived there and in the house next door for the next fourteen months while the negotiation process with the guerrillas played out. We were missionaries and not professional negotiators, so the U.S. Embassy provided two FBI specialists who coached us almost from day one. We knew from the three wives that the guerrillas (G's) had also taken the 2-way radio from Pucuro along with the three men, so we fully expected to hear from the captors. We set up our radio on the mission frequency and waited. On February 3, about 7:00 a.m., we received our first radio message—the G's wanted $5 million or our three men would be killed. After we got over the gut-wrenching shock, we told them that NTM had a *no ransom policy*. NTM would not pay a ransom payment to free our personnel. This is a policy that is common among most mission organizations.

The NTM team and our advisors assembled at the crisis center each morning by 6:30 a.m., never certain whether the G's would call us on the 2-way radio that day. We heard from them a number of times through March and into April—sometimes almost chummy; other times harsh and threatening. Our advisors warned us that it would be very bad news for us if the G's gave us a *deadline*—either pay-up by a certain date or our men would be killed. It would mean that they were prepared to draw a line in the sand, and to save face would not want to back down. That's exactly what happened on Good Friday morning, 1993. The message, though in Spanish, was very clear. They said, "Either pay us the money we are demanding or the day of Resurrection will be the day of the death of your men!"

We were all emotionally wrung out after the radio contact. I have never in my life been so distraught and felt so helpless. Our crisis teams of several couples prayed and talked, and strategized different responses—and prayed again! Why was God allowing this added heartache? Wasn't the kidnapping enough of a struggle for everyone? Why add to that the drama of a ransom deadline? I remember my wife and I going for walks on Easter Saturday and I still recall my throat being so tense that I felt like I had swallowed an apple whole. We talked at length with the U.S. Embassy staff and their advisors. We had no positive options at all!

In the end, we settled on a fairly simple plan. We felt that if we could somehow get past the actual deadline day without clear communication and into the following week, it could be enough of a distraction for the G's or give them an excuse, not to push the deadline.

As expected, the G's were right there on the 2-way radio, early on Easter Sunday morning. We determined that we would not have a clear radio contact with the G's no matter what. If we could convince them that we were experiencing bad weather in Panama City (they were undoubtedly in Colombia) through simulating static and radio interference, we might be able to get past this fearful day. It would take too long to detail here how we mimicked the sound of bad weather over the radio but suffice it to say that a bag of stale potato chips played a major role.

We never talked directly to the G's on that *day of Resurrection* and never really had a clear conversation with them until the following week. The G's never brought up the subject of the deadline and we sure didn't. We had about eighty radio conversations with the guerrillas in the year following the kidnapping. Then the radio went silent and there were no more calls.

I share all of the above to highlight the following spiritual principle. Just because Christians belong to Jesus Christ, it does not mean that He will run interference for us so that we don't experience any calamities. And even though He walks us through these times with His restful presence, there still is no guarantee that the outcome will be successful from our point of view. Let's remind ourselves again of the response of Shadrach, Meshach, and Abednego. "If it be so, our God whom we serve *is able to deliver us* from the furnace of blazing fire; and He will deliver us out of your hand, O King. But *even if He does not*, let it be known to you, O King, that we are not going to serve your gods (emphasis added)" (Daniel 3:17-18).

Let's think about the hostage situations in New Tribes Mission. God rescued the pilot, Paul Dye, in a miraculous way from Colombian guerrillas, but chose for other missionaries to die at the hands of their captors. Why the difference? Is it not this same principle of, "He is able to deliver us…but even if He does not." The bottom line can only be the sovereign will of our heavenly Father.

God's Word, the Bible, is good news from start to finish! It begins with the innocence of Eden and ends with the perfection of heaven. Yes, there is plenty of human tragedy and sadness due to sin between these two events. But what good news these pages contain! The sweetest truth to the spiritual palate is that it is all accomplished graciously by God out of His huge heart of love for mankind, in response to our faith in Him. Once we have received salvation as a free gift, the good news just keeps coming. At the time of salvation, Jesus Christ comes to take up residence in each one of His born again children and once again, in response to our faith in Him, He promises to live His divine life through our lives. And that, my brothers and sisters, is what Jesus calls *God's rest*! If that is not what you are experiencing, then why don't you follow Jesus' advice in the Gospel of Mark, chapter 6—*Come away and rest a while*!

CHAPTER THIRTEEN – THEMES FOR FURTHER STUDY

- Being a Christian does not exempt us from suffering. The Lord tells us up front that we can expect to suffer in this life just as He did on this earth. However, it will pale in comparison to the glory that Jesus has planned for us in heaven. (I Peter 1:20-21)

- The encouraging part of suffering is that Jesus is with us and *never* leaves us. (Hebrews 13:5,6)

- Shadrach, Meshach, and Abednego are thrown into the blazing furnace because of their loyalty to the God of Israel. The little phrase "if it be so" indicates that those who belong to God by faith in Him will at times face the fires of suffering, only because God has allowed it to be so. (Daniel 3:17)

- What a blessing to know that our heavenly Father is powerful enough to deliver us from *any* trial! (Jeremiah 32:27)

- Even when it appears that we are suffering because another person has control over us, we can rest in the truth that God is still in control—we are in His hands and He knows why He is allowing this trial. (Genesis 50:19-20)

- There are times when the Lord will go to miraculous ends to spare us pain and suffering; at other times He will appear to be doing nothing. Spiritual rest comes when we acknowledge that He is in control *all of the time*. (Hebrews 11:32-38)

APPENDIX

I think it would be valuable for the reader to be able to read all of the comments and answers to the five questions that I posed to the four widows. How did God reveal Himself to them personally in the midst of their excruciating experiences? God deals with each of His children differently and you and I will probably never face a scenario exactly like they faced. However, I believe it's important for us to hear firsthand how God reached out to these women during the deepest valleys of their lives and to be assured that His rest will be sufficient to carry us through our dark valleys also. I have used portions of their comments in previous chapters—here is the remainder of their poignant responses:

1. Could you describe any occasions during the kidnapping where, in the midst of feelings of fear, anxiety, doubt or disappointment with God, you clearly sensed His loving and caring presence? Did you have an assurance at these times that He was still in control of the circumstances? Would you describe this awareness as a time of spiritual rest?

   PATTI:
   "Many times during the hostage situation Nancy, Tania, and I needed to make unified decisions. I remember

one of us would make a statement and ask the others if we had a peace about that decision. If one answered 'No', then we would discuss it some more and only make a final decision when the three of us were in unity. Sometimes we prayed together to arrive at a decision.

"I think this all started on a trail to the river the day after our husbands were kidnapped. We were leaving the village and headed to the canoe when Estanislau ran up to us telling us that guerrilla footprints were spotted on the riverbank downriver. We froze! Looking from one to another and thinking the same thoughts, one of us asked, 'Should we stay in Pucuro another night or continue to leave?' I don't remember who said it first but we each answered saying, 'Yes, I have a peace about leaving.'

"Spiritual rest? I guess I would describe this as when I am experiencing peace. I believe that is when I am resting in the spirituality of God."

TANIA:

"During the kidnapping itself I was terrified. I don't remember having a sense that God was in control at the time. I just remember asking God for help and calmness and even when I didn't think I could keep doing what the guerrillas told me to do, I was able to keep following their orders. At the time, it just felt scary beyond belief but in hindsight, I can see that it was God giving me strength and answering my prayers. I can see how God directed my words that night and gave me grace to keep on going when I felt like giving up."

GRACIA:

"I can really identify with the Israelites who were going through the wilderness. Today, we read that story and think, 'Why can't you learn to not complain? Why can't you learn to trust Almighty God? Look at what He has done for you over and over.' But there in the jungle, it was a daily battle to trust again—to remind ourselves that He was in control again—because we forgot very quickly. I shouldn't say, '*We* forgot.' Martin seemed to be a better *rememberer* than me. I forgot very quickly. It was a daily battle with discouragement, doubt, despair, and worry. So, the spiritual rest of that day wore off quickly, if you know what I mean.

"I have to wonder if our captivity lasted as long as it did because I was a slow learner. By the end of our captivity, I think I had learned to trust God in a whole new way. I think the length of time between *days of despair* grew further and further apart as I began to change and began to trust that God had a plan and it was a good one and I just needed to be patient in the midst of it."

2. Hebrews 3 and 4 talk about *choosing* to enter into God's rest by faith, regardless of the situation. What did you find helped you the most when you felt that you were *losing it* spiritually, in order to enter back into God's rest?

TANIA:
"During the long years of waiting and not knowing, I feel like my life was mainly characterized by this very aspect of choosing to rest and trust. There were periods of time where life felt like a huge struggle. All looked black and hard. It felt like I had been abandoned by God at the time I needed Him most. It seemed like I would go through a cycle of intense struggle, doubt, fear, and sometimes anger until I was exhausted mentally, physically, and spiritually. Then, mainly out of desperation, I would tell God that I was giving up; that I couldn't do it anymore. All along this cycle I would be trying to walk with God and trust and rest, but it always seemed to come

down to this again. Next, there were times when I did just that for a while—I would give up and live defeated and depressed without joy. After that it seemed to come to a place where I didn't want to live like that anymore and this is where, for me, the real choice came."

3. Were there any aspects of *prayer* that God made very real to you during those intense emotional times associated with the kidnappings, that you really had not experienced prior to that time?

NANCY:
"As I look back at those nine years, I have to say that my prayer life was more of an SOS than a deep spiritual time. I was on stress overload and I believe that the prayers of the thousands of others were significantly deeper than my own. I also believe that God understood the 'Help me; I can't do this any longer. Help, God! I don't even know how to pray for Dave anymore.' I found that my prayer life had become a time of trying to put out the fires of the most urgent things that came into my life, but not much more."

PATTI:
"One time I was quoted as saying, 'I never say *Amen.*' I did say that because I felt like I was talking (praying) constantly with God; constantly, as in all the time. After the kidnapping, I felt like my prayer life was a 24 hours/7 days a week experience because I needed God so much in so many areas of my life. I took quiet time to listen to that still small voice and I feel that I experienced the knowledge of knowing God was always available to me. Before the kidnapping and sometimes today, I feel like my prayer life is a stop/go relationship. 'Okay, God, I

have time for you now.' Or, 'Okay, God, I need to tell you something, so listen to this.'"

TANIA:
"I think just praying about everything became crucial for me. Knowing that God knew and understood the deepest hurts of my heart and soul, even when I could not verbalize them, was incredibly comforting. I also experienced the power of others' prayers in a way I never had before. Many times after a sleepless night, some friend would call and tell me that they were awakened in the night and were burdened to pray for me. That was one of the little ways that God reminded me that He was still in control of the seeming chaos."

GRACIA:
"At one point—January or February—we were in a place for a long time—hiding out and lying low. We started getting wind that the military was near, but that there were some sort of negotiations going on. So, the Abu Sayyaf didn't want to move—they wanted to stay there. But we were hearing these rumors and it made us nervous. At one point—one evening as Martin was praying—he said something like this, 'Lord, we feel like we are in danger right now. If you have angels guarding us right now, would you just double the guard and grant us safety.' Martin had never prayed that way before. We tended to ask God for the safety we needed; we weren't the type to talk about guardian angels.

"That night I had to use the bathroom in the middle of the night. I put on my boots, got out of the hammock, and walked just a few steps away from the hammock. There wasn't much of a moon and I was afraid I would get disoriented and not be able to get back to the hammock if I went very far. Just before I went to the bathroom, I sensed a presence. I thought one of the guys might be up doing the same thing, so I just stood quietly and listened. I was going to wait until I knew I was alone. I didn't hear anything so I began looking around and I saw this big guy or maybe the shadow of a big guy, standing by a tree a ways away. Again, it was really dark and this was an uncharacteristically big guy. (Filipinos are very small people.) I waited, thinking that the angle of how I was seeing things made this guy look big and that he would move away. The guy never moved and I never heard anything more. It kind of freaked me out and after a while I just quickly did what I needed to and got back into the hammock. I awakened Martin and asked him to have a look since I had seen this big shadow. He got up, had a look, and reportedly didn't see anything. As I lay there in the hammock wondering about what I had seen, Martin's prayer that night came back to me, 'Would you just double the guard and grant us safety.' To this day, I wonder if I saw one of the *doubled guards*.

"To be quite honest, we saw lots of unanswered prayer during our captivity and I have to wonder about that. I have a lot of questions these days. I thought I had things figured out theologically before our captivity. I don't have many answers anymore, but I sure know the Lord like I never knew Him before! I guess it's better to know the Lord than to think you have your theology down pat. One of the verses I asked Martin about one day is from John 15:7. I asked, 'Why does Scripture say, "If you abide in Me, and My words abide in you, ask whatever you wish, and it shall be done for you?" Does that mean that we are not abiding in Christ if we are asking and our requests are not being granted—requests like us being rescued, or that the young girls in our group won't be mistreated, or that we would have enough food? It seems to me the Bible should have added a little clause there, "If you abide in Me and My words abide in you, ask whatever you wish, and if I agree to it and put my stamp of approval on it, it will be done unto you." Why doesn't it have that clause so God has an *out* and doesn't get blamed when we don't get our prayers answered?'"

4. What attribute of Jesus Christ's nature or personality provided the most comfort to you during the long stretches when the pain and intensity of your situation seemed to grind on and never come to a resolution?

NANCY:
"I began to realize that God didn't owe me anything. My life had been so blessed that without realizing it, I thought that as long as I was serving God and walking with Him, He would never allow anything bad to happen to me. But as I read the Scriptures, I realized that suffering was a big part of it. I began to understand that God promised to get us through suffering; not necessarily get us out of it! I had to get to the place where God alone was enough. God is love, whether I felt loved or not."

PATTI:
"Omniscience—knowing that God knew everything. I really think this helped me the most whenever I wondered about my future, the kids and their futures, life, ministry, the Kuna Indians and their futures, and family. Nothing I went through was a surprise to God. I just needed to draw strength from that and make Godly choices that had a positive eternal value."

TANIA:
"For me, it was God's faithfulness! Even though I doubted, accused, and was angry with God, He still loves me and will never give up on me."

GRACIA:
"It would have to be His love. We discussed a lot about who God is and what He is like when Martin and I talked together there in the jungle. When we debated the Abu Sayyaf, we would talk about God's justice and His mercy. We felt like we saw God extending His mercy and grace to us every day as well as to the members of the Abu Sayyaf. We hoped that the guerrillas would take advantage of those days of grace that were extended to them. We talked with them about God's holiness—His standard that both they and we knew could never be reached. The Muslims were very aware of their sin and their unworthiness before God. We agreed with them about God's omniscience, His being all powerful, His being the Creator and Ruler, and His judgment."

5. How did you actually apply verses of Scripture to be a help and encouragement to your own heart and mind during those darkest moments? What particular verses provided the most comfort to you?

NANCY:
"The following verse became my mainstay. It rang in my ears and was never far from my mind. Isaiah 41:10 says, 'Fear thou not; for I am with thee. Be not dismayed; for I am thy God. I will strengthen thee; yea, I will help thee; yea, I will uphold thee with the right hand of My righteousness (KJV)." I believe this verse provided me the most comfort during those years because it was my own fear that always loomed threateningly to draw me away from resting in the Lord. By quoting this verse over and over again in my mind, I was able to relinquish my fears to God and walk in His joy and peace once more."

PATTI:
"I remember one night; I'm pretty sure it was within the first six months. It was late and Dora (8 years old) still wasn't asleep. I climbed up into her bunk bed and lay down with her. She asked me, 'Mom, when daddy comes home, what if he doesn't want to be a missionary anymore? What if the Panamanian government won't let us back into the country?' The verse I shared with her was Philippians 4:8. 'The truth right now is that daddy isn't home. The truth right now is that God wants us to trust Him.' So I shared with Dora how we need to only focus on God and what was truth. That verse helped me many times during the years that followed.

"Philippians 4:13 also helped me in areas where I felt very insufficient for the task at hand. We three wives had many assignments and meetings over the course of those nine years. From Psalm 27:13-14, the key phrases were 'unless I had believed' and 'wait on the Lord.' Waiting is a very hard thing to do because there is no *doing* in it."

TANIA:
"I know this seems like a pat answer but the Psalms were a huge source of comfort—I was able to relate to the intensity of some of the Psalms in a new way. Also, Philippians and other epistles were a comfort. The bottom line is that the Bible is full of comfort and challenge; it became much more meaningful than it ever had been before."

GRACIA:
"Hebrews 12 means a lot to me. The race that is set before me is something totally different now; single parenting, speaking, and dealing with a bit of notoriety. These days, the sin that so easily besets me is, maybe, the mindless channel surfing with the remote when I just

don't feel like doing anything. But the encouragement is still the same. We look to Jesus, the author and finisher of our faith, who endured the cross for us and is sitting at the right hand of God. And the difference for me now is that I don't have to trust my memory! I can read the whole chapter and be encouraged to, 'Take a new grip with your tired hands (that used to hold mortars); stand firm on your shaky legs (Boy! Did they shake at the top of a hill!); and mark out a straight path for your feet. Then those who follow you, (my kids, those who hear me speak), though they are weak and lame, will not stumble and fall, but will become strong. (because they will be encouraged by what I saw God do for me)' NLT, verses 12, 13."

NOTES

Chapter One

1. Major W. Ian Thomas, *The Saving Life of Christ* (Grand Rapids: Zondervan, 1961).
2. *The Amplified Bible* (Grand Rapids: Zondervan, 1987), 1211.

Chapter Four

1. *Shane* – a 1953 western film made by Paramount Pictures, produced and directed by George Stevens.
2. Carrie Sydnor Coffman, *Weary Warriors* (La Crescenta: Apples of Gold, 1997), 37.
3. Ibid, 38.
4. Christina Maslach, *Burnout—The Cost of Caring* (Cambridge: Malor), 2.
5. *The Amplified Bible* (Grand Rapids: Zondervan, 1987), 1324.

Chapter Six

1. *The New Scofield Reference Bible, Holy Bible, Authorized King James Version* (New York: Oxford, 1967), 1010.

Chapter Seven

1. Durant Imboden, *Durant Imboden's Europe For Visitors*, from Hampton Court Palace Gardens, www.europeforvisitors.com
2. *The Amplified Bible* (Grand Rapids: Zondervan, 1987), 1348-1349.

Chapter Eight

1. *The Amplified Bible* (Grand Rapids: Zondervan, 1987), 1236.
2. Ibid, 1236.

Chapter Nine

1. *The Amplified Bible* (Grand Rapids: Zondervan, 1987), 849.

Chapter Ten

1. *The Amplified Bible* (Grand Rapids: Zondervan, 1987), 1427.
2. *The New Scofield Reference Bible, Holy Bible, Authorized King James Version* (New York: Oxford, 1967), 1313.
3. Personal conversation with Nancy (Mankins) Hamm on 6/12/2007.
4. Nancy Mankins, *Hostage* (Nashville: W. Publishing Group, 2001).

Chapter Eleven

1. *The Amplified Bible* (Grand Rapids: Zondervan, 1987), 1365.

2. Major W. Ian Thomas, *The Saving Life of Christ* (Grand Rapids: Zondervan, 1961), 18.
3. *The Amplified Bible* (Grand Rapids: Zondervan, 1987), 1365.
4. Major W. Ian Thomas, *The Saving Life of Christ* (Grand Rapids: Zondervan, 1961), 100.
5. *The Amplified Bible* (Grand Rapids: Zondervan, 1987), 1429.

Chapter Twelve

1. *The New Scofield Reference Bible, Holy Bible, Authorized King James Version* (New York: Oxford, 1967), 1314.

Chapter Thirteen

1. *The Amplified Bible* (Grand Rapids: Zondervan, 1987), 1308.

Printed in the United States
213668BV00002B/2/P